...tten last Monday gave some ...
...ments and those of the b...
...day upon these pages & when ...
...them home—

...k to Floyd's camp where I last ...
...Wise's camp, & the whole rege...
...with indignation at the man...
...urs were treated by the two legio...
...tinually.—We were told that ...
...hing to attack Floyd; but did ...
...ole affair a false alarm.
...nt was but in motion. We ...

CIVIL WAR CHRONICLES

A SOLDIER'S STORY

CIVIL WAR CHRONICLES

A SOLDIER'S STORY

David Phillips

MetroBooks

An Imprint of Friedman/Fairfax Publishers

© 1997 by Michael Friedman Publishing Group, Inc.

Library of Congress Cataloging-in-Publication Data available upon request.

ISBN 1-56799-425-3

Editor: Nathaniel Marunas
Art Director: Kevin Ullrich
Designer: Garrett Schuh
Photography Editor: Kathryn Culley
Production Manager: Camille Lee

Color separations by Bright Arts (Singapore) Pte. Ltd.
Printed in China by Leefung-Asco Printers Ltd.

1   3   5   7   9   10   8   6   4   2

For bulk purchases and special sales, please contact:
Friedman/Fairfax Publishers
Attention: Sales Department
15 West 26th Street
New York, NY 10010
(212) 685-6610 FAX (212) 685-1307

Visit our website:
http://www.metrobooks.com

DEDICATION

As might be expected, promising leads regarding the wartime activities of Isaac Smith, Christopher and Ellen Tompkins, and John P. Hale often led nowhere because the espionage undertaken by these people was never documented. What little information there was had to be deduced from relatively innocent sources, such as Christopher Tompkins' postwar paper about the fall of Richmond. Fortunately, there was one player in this history who kept my interest at a high pitch.

The courageous Ellen Tompkins—a woman who later denied any knowledge of the Civil War when questioned by her grandchildren—worked quietly to support her husband and the cause they both supported. Although she verbally denied any knowledge of warfare, her letters reveal a solid grasp of military matters, the probable recruitment of a local postmaster into her ring of spies, and the use of a clandestine message system that relied on the U.S. postal service and a Confederate courier system. She risked her life, property, and the safety of her children to support her adopted state, Virginia.

This brave woman was instrumental in the success of her husband's undertakings, and readers should pause to remember her inspiring example.

ACKNOWLEDGMENTS

It would have been impossible to write this account without the solid support of two wonderful people.

Without the excellent research of Rebecca L. Hill, this book might never have happened. It was her tenacious searches through poorly indexed, obscure records that brought the fascinating people in this history to life.

Equal credit must be given to my patient and wonderful wife, Sue A. Phillips, who encouraged me to continue writing when early leads seemed to hold nothing but frustration in store.

CONTENTS

INTRODUCTION
Clandestine Intelligence Operations in Civil War Virginia

Isaac Noyes Smith's Civil War experiences came to light after a close reading of a short monograph on the fall of Richmond that had been written by Christopher Quarles Tompkins, a Confederate officer who was the primary organizer of Confederate forces in Virginia's western counties. Tompkins had written about the loss of two of his mules to a soldier fleeing from the Union army who had politely written him a pencil note that stated that the young man regretted the necessity of impressing the mules into his service. The young man signed his name Jas. N. Snead. In writing of this incident, Tompkins expressed his astonishment that the young man could be so naive as to sign his name in such a fashion.

It was this simple note that led to the slow unraveling of the Civil War activities of Isaac N. Smith, an extraordinary Confederate soldier who resigned from the active service of his state and eventually entered into its clandestine service.

There was no known connection between Smith and Snead, but there was a connection between the names—one that was obvious to former Confederate colonel Tompkins. Tompkins had served as the commander of Virginia's 22nd Infantry Regiment during the early stages of the Civil War. Light research revealed his relationship with Major Isaac Smith, who had served as Tompkins' deputy in the 22nd Virginia. The serious part of the research began as a connection was

"Even the leaders of the Unionists found their own 'house divided against itself,' for scarce one of them but had a son in Wise's Legion and the Twenty-second Virginia Regiment was largely composed of the young men of Charleston and the vicinity."

—Jacob D. Cox, on the Union sympathizers in western Virginia

PAGE 9: A graduate of prestigious Washington College, Isaac Smith was a respected attorney who had represented his region in Richmond. Nonetheless, like many other young professionals from his region he first served the Confederacy as a private (he became a major in the 22nd Virginia later on during the Civil War). ABOVE: As a resident of the area near Gauley Bridge, Christopher Q. Tompkins (pictured here late in life) became an early organizer of Virginia's forces in the Kanawha Valley. As commander of the 22nd Virginia Infantry Regiment, he was Isaac Smith's friend and military mentor. RIGHT: This hastily sketched but informative map is featured in Smith's diary. It was among the detailed entries Major Smith made in a diary—cast as an extended letter to his wife— that he maintained during his service under General John B. Floyd. The map shows the battle-field at Carnifex Ferry and explains the move-ments of his regiment during and after the battle.

sought between the names Jas N. Snead and Isaac N. Smith.

"I" and "J" were handwritten the same way during this period, which made the ini-tials of the two names the same, suggesting of course that they were one and the same

man. But why did Tompkins think this was naive? After long months of research, the answer was located. Tompkins was manag-ing a spy network of an undetermined size under cover of a commercial occupation, the Tredegar Arms Works in Richmond, and

Smith was one of his primary agents. This was the man fleeing from the Union army following the fall of Richmond in 1865 in need of mules. The spy master felt it was naive for his agent to use an alias that had the same initials as his true name.

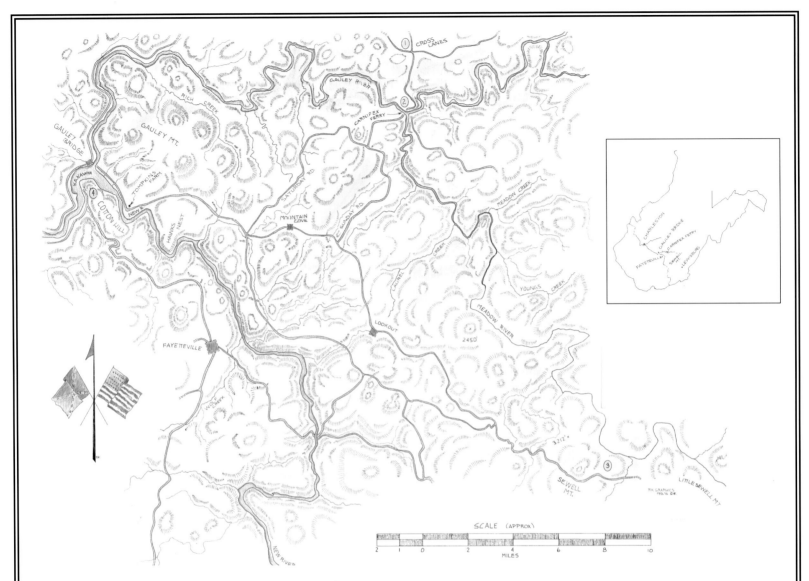

NEW RIVER AND GAULEY RIVER AREA OF OPERATIONS (AUGUST–NOVEMBER 1861)—OVERHEAD VIEW

This map shows the areas of operations discussed in this book. The terrain markings give an indication of the intrinsic strategic difficulties involved in the campaigns in western Virginia.

1. Battle of Cross Lanes (August 26, 1861). Confederate forces under General John B. Floyd surprise and route the 7th Ohio.

2. Battle of Carnifex Ferry (September 10, 1861). Union forces under General William S. Rosecrans attack Floyd's camp at Carnifex Ferry. During the night of September 10, Confederate forces fall back across the Gauley River to Sewell Mountain.

3. Sewell Mountain (September–October 1861). Union forces pursue the Confederate "retrograde movement" to Sewell Mountain, which has two peaks. Confederates establish earthworks and a camp on the eastern peak; Union troops occupy the western peak. On October 6, after an inconclusive confrontation, Union forces withdraw and move to the Gauley Bridge area.

4. Siege of Gauley Bridge (November 1–7, 1861). Confederates shell Union positions at Gauley Bridge from across the Kanawha River and at Kanawha Falls from Cotton Hill.

This mountaineer's but in western Virginia was typical of the crude residences of the rural inhabitants of the narrow mountain valleys. Farming plots were small and the manual labor required just to eke out a meager living was grueling.

Settlers moved into the rugged Appalachian Mountains only after the flatter, more arable land in eastern Virginia had already been occupied. Unfortunately, the small plots that were available did not support large-scale agriculture. As a result, there was a limited need for slaves in the region.

Smith wasn't the only former member of Tompkins' regiment who resigned his commission and entered Virginia's clandestine service. John P. Hale, an artillery commander who had served under Tompkins, also resigned early in the war, but later accepted "a special commission for a special purpose, from the government," as related in a letter from Smith to Tompkins. "Special commission" was almost certainly a euphemism for espionage. Hale, a part of the ring in which Smith operated, resigned from the Confederate army in the summer of 1861, but he was operating a steamboat line that ran between Charleston and Cincinnati in 1863. By 1864, Hale was involved in the construction of a boat in Buffalo, New York—a rather farflung commercial venture for a former Confederate officer—that provided an excellent cover for his "special commission" from the Confederate government.

Smith's fascinating story showed the complexity of the lives of people living in Virginia's western counties as the Civil War loomed. Western Virginians lived in a region that was also a border territory. These counties were later to secede from Virginia to form a new state, West Virginia. Isaac Smith's personal and military life became more complex than those of many of his contemporaries when it became known that his father was a prominent Unionist who was taking a lead in the "new State Movement" in Virginia—a traitor in the eyes of the Confederate army. It was a time of great passion, and Smith was to bear the brunt of a great amount of personal pain associated with these passions.

The period between the end of the Mexican War and the outbreak of the Civil War was a difficult time for nearly everyone living in the United States. Two distinct geographical sections based on different cultures were emerging and each in its way contended for dominance of the entire nation. Not surprisingly, both North and South began to fear that it would fall under the domination of the other. It was, however, in the border

regions lying between the two contending sections that political unrest and turmoil began to have its greatest impact as differing political beliefs within small communities erupted into family feuds.

The fate of the nation was being debated in the Congress of the United States, where a precarious balance between "free" and "slave" states existed. Political compromise after compromise followed the loud and extended arguments between the partisans of both sides as they debated whether the states to be formed from territories captured from Mexico would be free or slave states. Fear dominated the national scene as northerners began to call for an end to slavery while southerners defended the practice, which was the underpinning of their economy.

Events began to take a violent turn as militant abolitionist John Brown began to mobilize in Kansas, a border area that was contested by both sides. Brown and a few of his followers were involved in the murder of several proslavery Kansas settlers. Brown and his followers then moved their operation to southern Maryland. Equipped with long pikes with which to arm the slaves they managed to free, Brown and his men attacked and occupied the Federal armory at Harpers Ferry, Virginia. They were soon surrounded by local militia and Federal Marines under the command of Robert E. Lee and J.E.B. Stuart, who attacked and captured Brown's party. The trial of Brown in a Virginia State court, the display of the weapons, and his intention to incite slaves against their masters aggravated the volatile national situation. Virginians had experienced a slave uprising (Nat Turner's Rebellion) and this memory was fresh in the minds of young Virginians, who consequently rushed to enlist in local militia companies formed to defend their families from raiders like Brown.

Isaac Noyes Smith was a member of a militia company formed in Charleston in Virginia's western counties. He served with a group of other volunteers in the Kanawha Riflemen as a private—even though he was a member of a prominent family, an attorney who had studied at the prestigious Washington College in Lexington, Virginia, and had served for two years as a member of the Virginia legislature in Richmond. This very unusual private was soon elected by the

John Brown was an ardent, eloquent, and militant abolitionist who used extreme measures to protest the inhumane practice of slavery. His passion led him to back several proslavery men to death in Kansas. He later attacked the weapons depot at Harpers Ferry, an event that in many ways set the stage for the Civil War.

members of his regiment to become a major, second only to Colonel Tompkins, who became his friend and mentor.

Fighting soon came to the region as the Union army invaded western Virginia. Smith's commander in chief, a militarily illiterate former governor of Virginia, ordered his western volunteers into a "retrograde movement," a retreat that left most of the soldiers' families under the control of the Federal army. The newly married Smith was forced by military necessity to leave his wife and parents to the Union forces as he prepared to fight to defend the homes of the eastern Virginians.

The story of this soldier, a man with clearly conflicting duties, is one of the more intriguing tales to emerge from the Civil War.

This illustration shows a slave gang being moved from eastern Virginia to Kentucky. During the antebellum period large numbers of slaves were shipped from the prosperous eastern region of Virginia to new plantations throughout the South, but few were ever purchased by farmers in the small fields of nearby western Virginia.

chapter 1

A COUNTRY LURCHES TOWARD WAR

Free at last I hope—restored to civilization once more. Out of the army and comfortably housed and fed. You can scarcely conceive the intense relief and enjoyment of my freedom. Not a soldier within twenty miles [32km] of me and the army forty miles [64km] away. Unless I am persecuted by Floyd's malignity upon false pretenses and without a shadow of right of law—I am again a white man.

The young soldier Isaac Noyes Smith made this entry in his diary on November 20, 1861, in celebration of his release from an oath of allegiance he had made to the Confederate army several months earlier.

Campaigning throughout many of what were then the counties of western Virginia, the young man's outlook on the Civil War had altered as the fortunes of the Confederacy began to wane on the western slopes of the Allegheny Mountains. From a period of jubilation and confidence, the supporters of what they felt was a second American Revolution had begun to despair. Smith had come to feel both persecution and injustice at the hands of his commander; the above quote shows the young man's relief at being freed from what he had come to consider a form of slavery.

Smith's fascinating story rises from the political turmoil that followed John Brown's attack on Harpers Ferry—a raid launched on Virginia soil with the goal of securing free-

"This war was never really contemplated in earnest. I believe if either the North or the South had expected that their differences would result in this obstinate struggle, the cold-blooded Puritan and the cock-hatted Huguenot and Cavalier would have made a compromise."

—George E. Pickett, June 27, 1862

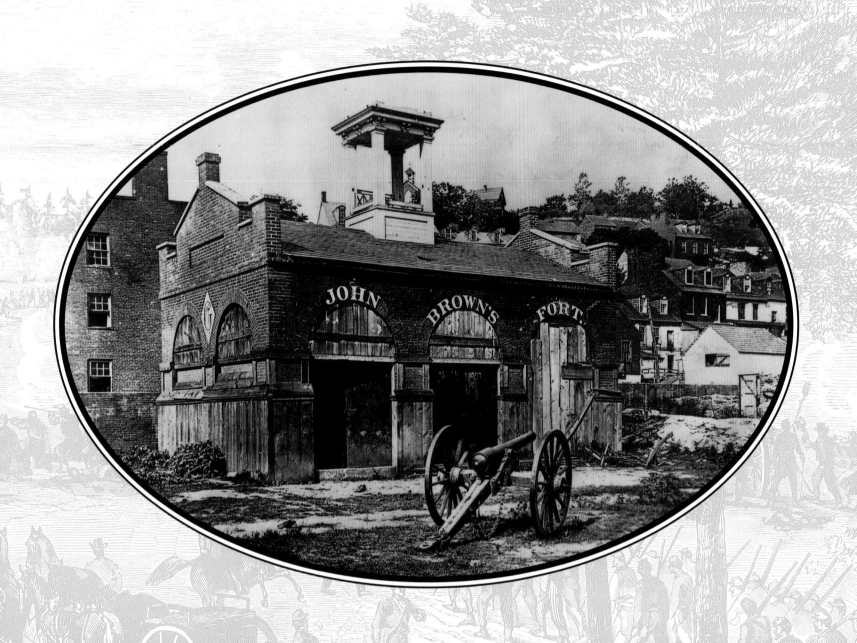

PAGE 15: John Brown's "fort" was a firehouse on the Harpers Ferry arsenal grounds. Brown and his men barricaded themselves within the building until they were subdued and arrested by a group of U.S. Marines under the temporary command of two army officers on leave from their respective regiments: Robert E. Lee and J.E.B. Stuart. ABOVE: John Brown's subsequent execution in Charlestown, Virginia, came at the end of a state trial that was followed closely around the young nation, broadening the gap separating pro- and antislavery forces.

dom for the slaves of the South. In the aftermath of the fighting, young men in Virginia rushed to enlist in volunteer militia units, and units that already existed began to drill, perfecting their military skills. There was a fear among southerners that northern extremists would soon launch another attack with the intention of arming slaves, who would then begin killing whites (as had happened during Virginia's Nat Turner Rebellion). Both concern for the safety of their families and loyalty to their states (as opposed to a nationalistic loyalty) drew the young men to join the new volunteer companies as they were formed, and the oaths these young men took would serve to bind them to their units as the next phase of the conflict—secession—unfolded.

The diarist, Major Isaac Smith, had become a soldier in the volunteer service of the state of Virginia. At the time, Virginia was known both as the "Mother of States," due to the large number of emigrants from Virginia who had gone on to found new states, and the "Mother of Presidents," because half of the presidents up to that point in the nation's brief history had come from Virginia. Volunteering to defend the sovereignty and freedom of one's state was viewed as an honorable, if not mandatory, act on the part of southern gentlemen of the period. Because of their state's particular importance, many Virginian gentlemen—among them Smith—felt especially honorbound to defend their state.

On closer examination, however, these sentiments were not ubiquitously held in Virginia because different sections of the vast region had significantly different views on the social and economic issues that were dividing the nation. There were many blacks living in slavery in Virginia's eastern counties, which afforded the members of the white upper class the leisure time to engage in nearly limitless social activities. The western Virginians, in contrast to their eastern cousins, owned few slaves because their small farms would not support large-scale agriculture; as a result these men and women spent most of their time working. They had little leisure time for anything other than regular attendance to church services. As a result of these varied lifestyles, a substantial political rift developed between the two regions.

The western Virginians complained constantly that they were not represented fairly in Richmond, the state capital. For instance, the state constitution, ratified in 1776, allowed for two representatives from each county, but since there were more counties in the east, westerners felt that representation should be based on the total white population. Since they lacked adequate representation at Richmond, westerners felt they were denied their fair share of state-funded developments, including state banks and other internal improvements. At the time, there were macadamized highways in Virginia's eastern valleys—one ran the length of the Shenandoah Valley—but western cities had dirt and mud streets.

The right to vote in Virginia was also a serious issue. The state constitution required that only those citizens possessing twenty-five acres (10ha) of land could be allowed to vote, but there were few places in the western counties where twenty-five acres (10ha) of flat land could be located in a single parcel because of the mountainous terrain.

Virginia's voting population in 1830 numbered just under fifty thousand out of a total population of about 600,000. Because the majority of these voters lived in the state's eastern counties, western Virginians had little hope of ever securing control of their affairs.

Additionally, the differences between the two regions of Virginia were not limited to politics. Well-established Episcopalians, Baptists, Methodists, and Presbyterians had a long association with the practice of slavery and fully accepted it as an institution. While the westerners were often associated with these same religious branches, some worshiped in Quaker, Mennonite, and Dunkard congregations that included many recent immigrants who had had limited experience with slavery and were less likely to support

it. Some of the persistent differences over slavery could not be reconciled within the churches. One group, the Methodists, actually split into two separate camps over the slavery question in 1846, and the boundary line that separated the two closely followed the border of the new state that was soon to be created during the Civil War: West Virginia.

While the western Virginians were generally opposed to slavery, it was not through excessive interest in the humanitarian treatment of the black population that created this opposition. Most of them felt the presence of slaves meant that there would be fewer and fewer basic employment opportunities through which enterprising young white men could begin the process of

This view of western Virginia's mountains clearly illustrates the difficulty facing any military strategist contemplating operations among the region's many peaks and valleys. The rugged terrain combined with terrible weather conditions made it a miserable location for a campaign, and the soldiers of both Union and Rebel forces suffered considerably.

Slaves performed most of the manual labor on large agricultural plantations in the South, but the majority of small farmers and individual white laborers resented it because the utilization of slaves filled most entry-level agricultural jobs and blocked poor whites from acquiring even the most basic employment. This situation was particularly tense in Virginia, which was a state divided against itself.

personal development that could eventually lead to prosperity. Western Virginians believed that slavery slowed the process of economic development and they did not support the practice.

This was the political environment in which Major Isaac Smith developed. He had become a lawyer, like his father, and was one of Charleston's many young aristocrats who was drawn to service in a local military unit, in Smith's case under the command of a man named George S. Patton.

A graduate of Virginia's Military Institute, Patton—whose grandson would become famous in World War II—had originally organized his volunteer militia in 1856 and named it the Kanawha Minutemen. The unit was patterned after the well-known Richmond Light Infantry Blues and met, drilled, and participated in local fairs to

George S. Patton, the grandfather of General Patton of World War II fame, served in the 22nd Virginia with Isaac Smith. Patton would lose his life at Winchester in 1864.

demonstrate the volunteers' skill at marching and drilling with their rifles. The name was changed in 1859, and the local company came to be known as the Kanawha Riflemen at the time of the raid on Harpers Ferry by John Brown and his supporters.

Isaac Smith served under George S. Patton in both incarnations of the volunteer unit as a private—in spite of the fact that he had a university degree, was a practicing attorney, and had served a term as state legislator in Richmond, where he represented the interests of the people of the western region. Several other attorneys from the area also served in the volunteer company, entering into Virginia's service soon after the outbreak of hostilities at Fort Sumter, South Carolina. These educated young men proved to be good raw material for drill instructors as political tensions between North and

Fort Sumter became a violent flashpoint when South Carolina's forces demanded a surrender of the Federal garrison there. The attack prompted President Lincoln to call for seventy-five thousand volunteers to suppress the rebellion. Fort Sumter is depicted here following a Federal bombardment in 1863.

Harpers Ferry, Virginia, was the site of a Federal armory during the prewar years. John Brown's attack on the facility—his intention was to arm African Americans so that they could liberate themselves—set into motion a sequence of events that further polarized an already troubled nation.

A COUNTRY LURCHES TOWARD WAR

South began to intensify. Virginia had attempted to remain neutral as both sides began to arm, but this was to be in vain. When, facing a rebellion on a huge scale, President Lincoln called for additional troops—a total of seventy-five thousand men—to suppress "combinations too powerful to be suppressed by the ordinary course of judicial proceedings or by the powers vested in the marshals by law," Virginians began to leave the Union.

The men serving under Captain George S. Patton quickly declared their intentions with regard to Lincoln's call to arms: "We, the Kanawha Riflemen, hereby declare it to be our fixed purpose to never use arms against the state of Virginia, or any other southern state, in any attempt to coerce or subjugate them. That we hereby tender our

services to the authorities of the state, to be used in the emergency contemplated."

Like these Virginian volunteers, young men across the South were preparing for war against the northern invaders that they expected to enter their home territory from the states choosing to remain loyal to the Union. Most (if not all) of these young men were completely unprepared for the events that would soon engulf them. In the volunteer unit under Patton, the men continued their preparations. A few veterans of the Mexican War—and soon after, West Point graduate Christopher Q. Tompkins—would enter these volunteers' lives, Tompkins as the local commander of Virginia's western forces.

Amateur soldiers from all over the western counties began to assemble in the lower Kanawha Valley, from which they hoped to

Robert E. Lee was felt to be one of the most talented officers in the country during the prewar period. Despite his personal charisma and considerable skills as a leader and strategist, combat in Virginia's western mountains would age him considerably.

be able to defend Virginia's frontier with Ohio (along the 250-mile [402km] Ohio River front). The well-drilled Kanawha Riflemen probably served as instructors for the newly arriving men who were eagerly volunteering for service in the ranks of Virginia's defenders.

As the Virginians suspected, the time was approaching when their state's western counties would come under attack. Ohio's recently organized strategists had quickly evaluated their maps and begun to make plans for an invasion that was to be the first stage in a larger offensive against Richmond that (it was hoped) would end the war. Two things made the western part of Virginia the appropriate first target for the Ohio units. First, the Baltimore & Ohio Railroad (which crossed western Virginia) was a transportation artery the Union needed to control if they were to

The Baltimore & Ohio Railroad was one of the critical transportation links connecting the Union's Midwest with the East Coast. The loss of control of the railroad would have forced the Union army to lengthen its already overextended supply line. Accordingly, the Union sought to secure the railway immediately following the outbreak of hostilities.

Colonel George Porterfield and his untrained Virginians have the dubious distinction of losing the first land battle of the Civil War, at Philippi, Virginia.

operating in the northern end of the Shenandoah Valley and strike directly toward Richmond to end the war. Also, as this force moved into Virginia, the defenders would have to respond to its presence by splitting their forces. A similar Federal force would move across the Baltimore & Ohio Railroad, secure it, and become the force in the Shenandoah Valley that would combine with the regiments arriving along the Kanawha Valley route. The plan was a good one, and Ohio soldiers began to move from their training camps to the shore of the Ohio River. Ohio's General George McClellan would command the primary thrust into Confederate territory along the vital Baltimore & Ohio Railroad while his subordinate, General Jacob D. Cox, would command the Federal army scheduled to move along the Kanawha River route.

Virginia's troops had to respond to these simultaneous threats, so the volunteer regiments began to muster. Patrols in the vicinity of the Ohio River began to report Federal troop movements and thus the stage was set for combat. On a larger scale, certain strategic decisions had been made by the politicians of the new Confederacy that would cast the southern forces in a very definite role throughout the war. By concentrating the military forces of the South on the defense of their borders, the Confederates became the defenders—a role they would play with few exceptions for the duration of the war. By the same token, the North was cast in the role of the aggressor. Throughout

be able to move large numbers of troops and military supplies from the Midwest to the East Coast. Second, the rivers of western Virginia also provided a route for the transportation of troops through the region.

The Great Kanawha River is broad, deep, and navigable by even large steamboats for much of its length. Flowing from the foot of the western edge of the Allegheny Mountains at the small town of Gauley Bridge, where New River joins the Gauley River—both of which tumble from the high mountains—to form the Kanawha, this broad stream offered opportunities to military strategists in Ohio. Troops could travel easily aboard large riverboats to the river's head, unload, and march across the mountains along the James River and Kanawha Turnpike. Once across the mountains, it would be a relatively simple measure to combine with other Union forces

The Battle of Rich Mountain was won on June 12, 1861, by William S. Rosecrans after a sympathetic young civilian from the region offered to lead Federal infantry to his father's farm, located to the rear of the Confederate defenders.

These pickets on the main turnpike near the hamlet of Gauley Bridge were armed with sabers as well as rifles. In all likelihood these men were part of a Virginia cavalry regiment.

the war Union forces would attack and the Confederate forces would defend, and it was no different as Ohio regiments moved into western Virginia.

The primary players in the Virginia conflict did not approach their military duties with enthusiasm. Most of the soldiers on both sides shared the belief that any fighting would be brief and that a short campaign would end the fighting. As the soldiers of both sides came into close proximity, small fights began to develop. On May 22, 1861, a small Union scouting party in the vicinity of the Baltimore & Ohio Railroad encountered secessionist pickets where the Northwestern Turnpike crossed the railroad. Shots were fired and one Union soldier, Private Thornsberry Bailey Brown, was struck in the chest by three musket balls and died. He became the first Union combat casualty of the war.

Additional forces moved into the region. General Robert E. Lee, serving as commander of Virginia's state forces, sent a small, untrained, and underequipped force under Colonel George Porterfield to occupy the town of Grafton, but pressure from assembling Federal troops forced Porterfield to withdraw to the town of Philippi, where he was surprised on June 3 by a large Union force under Colonel Benjamin F. Kelley. There were no deaths in this fighting and few soldiers were wounded—Kelley, who was shot in the chest, was one of them—but the first land battle of the Civil War had been fought.

General George B. McClellan moved across the Ohio River on June 21 with twenty thousand soldiers and began a short maneuver campaign, the first of the Civil War. Battles would be fought at Cheat Mountain, Rich Mountain, and Corrick's Ford, producing small Union victories against the new Confederate army. These victories were widely reported in northern newspapers,

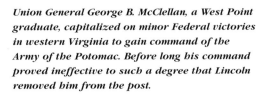

Union General George B. McClellan, a West Point graduate, capitalized on minor Federal victories in western Virginia to gain command of the Army of the Potomac. Before long his command proved ineffective to such a degree that Lincoln removed him from the post.

Confederate officer Albert Gallatin Jenkins formed the Border Rangers early in the war and served as a cavalry commander until he was mortally wounded in a conflict at Cloyd's Mountain in 1864.

Henry A. Wise, a former governor of Virginia, was commissioned as a Confederate brigadier general to command Virginia's troops in the western Virginia theater.

enabling McClellan to grab national attention and undoubtedly leading to the call to assume the command of the entire Union army on July 22, following the loss at Bull Run.

The second campaign, under the command of Jacob Cox, began in early July. By July 11, the troops were moving across the river and had entered into Virginia. Cox was a lawyer who had been active in the formation of the Republican party in Ohio, was a member of a small antislavery group that also included future president James A. Garfield, and served as a militia general. He was a reluctant soldier who was determined to do his duty; he learned the art of the soldier as he managed large numbers of men entering into combat. He described his feel-

ings poignantly: "I went about my duties with a half-choking sense of grief I dared not think of."

Cox moved his small army upstream on the Kanawha River aboard riverboats as his scouting parties moved ahead on either shore. Should the scouts discover an enemy presence, Cox would be able to land fresh, rested troops to mount an attack. It was a leisurely way to start a war, but the Unionist citizens living along the river nevertheless cheered and waved flags as they passed. But the citizenry of the area was far from being uniform in its sympathies.

Virginia's defenders were also in motion. The men of the Border Rangers, serving under Albert Gallatin Jenkins, moved toward likely defensive positions and with the assistance of some local militia engaged in a

brief fight with Cox's 2nd Kentucky at Barboursville on July 12. The Union regiments formed several columns as they began to march upon the Confederates. Because the Union columns were mutually supporting, however, the outnumbered Virginians fell back, then slowly began to assemble additional strength.

Cox united his columns, and on July 17 sent the 12th Ohio with two companies of the 21st Ohio to make a landing at Scary Creek. The Confederate pickets were quickly uprooted by the advancing Ohio soldiers, but two of the Union charges were driven back with casualties. As a third attack was being prepared, Confederate reinforcements arrived on the field and the Union soldiers broke ranks and fled to the rear.

The Confederate commander on the field, George S. Patton, was seriously wounded in the shoulder so Albert Jenkins assumed command. Sensing that Union forces were regrouping for a third attempt to penetrate the line, Jenkins promptly ordered the men to withdraw. Having halted the Union forces, the Confederates later returned to the field and claimed victory, the first for the southern forces in the Civil War.

Fourteen Federal soldiers were killed, thirty were wounded, and twenty-one were declared missing, while five Confederate soldiers were killed and twenty-six wounded. Some Union soldiers were captured in the confusion at the end of the fight as both sides withdrew from the field. James Sedinger, a Confederate cavalryman who participated in the fight, described a comic scene:

Our company mounted their horses and rode over to where the Yankee line of battle was on top of the hill near Mrs. Simm's house. While sitting there a Col. Woodruff, Col. Devillius [DeVilliers], and their staff rode up to Capt. Jenkins and said to him, 'Well, you have given the Rebels a good thrashing today,' [whereupon Jenkins] ordered them to surrender which they did with considerable grumbling. It was twilight and they could not distinguish our uniforms from theirs.

Meanwhile, General McClellan's forces operating in the region of the Baltimore & Ohio Railroad were able to defeat Confederate General Garnett at Rich Mountain. As a result, the Confederates were faced with the clear danger that one of McClellan's subordinates, General William S. Rosecrans, would move south and occupy Gauley Bridge, the strategic town at the junction of New and Gauley Rivers, and effectively trap the small Confederate army operating in the Kanawha Valley against Cox.

The Confederate commander, General Henry A. Wise, a former governor of Virginia

Confederate General John B. Floyd served in the Buchanan administration as Secretary of War. With a commission that predated that of Wise, Floyd assumed command from his colleague in western Virginia once he arrived.

Henry Heth served with Floyd in the Kanawha Valley campaign of 1861. A West Point graduate, Heth (pronounced "Heath") probably served as a military advisor to Floyd.

who had gained some degree of fame as well as notoriety through his management of the John Brown trial, ordered a "retrograde movement," a retreat, into the mountainous region of Fayette and Greenbrier counties. Crossing the barrier of Gauley River as he entered the mountains, Wise ordered his men to burn the 520-foot (158m) covered bridge on July 27 as Cox's advance regiments approached. This effectively halted this phase of the Union campaign. Cox was at the limit of his supply line and the wide, rushing river slowed his men at last. The earlier destruction of bridges by Wise's small army as it retreated had slowed Cox down by only a few hours. Cox had an engineer in his 11th Ohio Infantry Regiment, Philander P. Lane, who with mechanics in his regiment was able to rebuild the bridges as their piers

cooled. But the high banks, swift water, and great width of the Gauley River prevented Lane from rebuilding the bridge immediately. He chose instead to build a ferry, which Cox used to transport a few companies across the river and into the mountains, where they were instructed to conduct aggressive patrols to give Wise the impression that the Federal force was larger than it actually was.

Cox was aware that he was now in a difficult position. Although an amateur soldier, Cox was a quick learner and had realized that the commander who conquers territory must secure it with garrisons to protect the lines of communication with the base. Consequently, as a commander won territory, he lost strength. As Wise pulled back—trading space for time in a classic maneuver—he was moving nearer to his base and shortening his supply line. Also, the Confederates

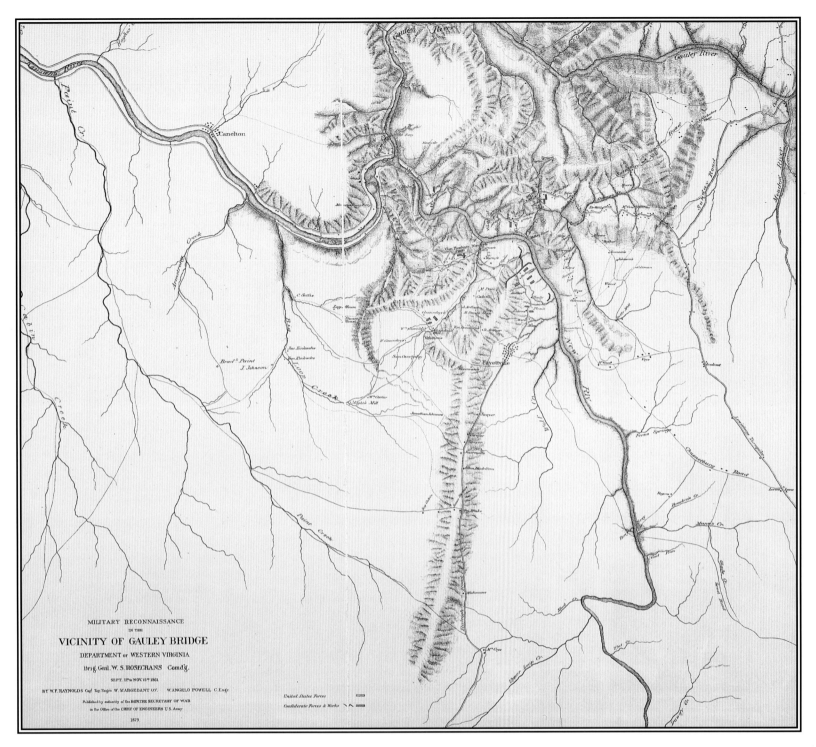

This map of the Gauley Bridge area clearly shows the rugged terrain over which the contending forces had to operate during the summer and autumn of 1861. Federal forces under Jacob D. Cox were able to occupy Gauley Bridge, but once the long covered bridge across Gauley River was destroyed by fire, Cox's extended supply line was unable to support any further advance into the mountains to the east.

After its destruction by fire, Gauley Bridge was rebuilt by the Union army with a prefabricated structure in twenty-eight days, in early 1862. It was in use until September 1862, when retreating Union soldiers destroyed it again.

Gauley Bridge, lying on the western side of the rugged Gauley River, was a major supply depot for the Union army throughout most of the Civil War. In this illustration, the small hamlet is surrounded by Federal Sibley tents; the piers of the destroyed bridge support a temporary ferry.

were assembling additional forces with which to oppose any future moves by Cox. The net effect was that Cox's position was becoming weaker by the day while his opponent was receiving reinforcements.

Unfortunately, these reinforcements also created a new set of problems for the Confederates, because with the additional troops came a new commander, John B. Floyd, who was also a former governor of Virginia and a political rival of Wise. The invading Union army continued to push Wise's Confederate forces into the mountains to the east, where they were soon to make contact with the new reinforcements arriving into the region under the command of Floyd.

As the Confederate army was pushed out of the Kanawha Valley, the officers and men who had volunteered to serve were moving farther from their homes and families. Most had volunteered with the understanding that they were enrolling into volunteer units formed specifically to defend the region in which they lived. Not surprisingly, large numbers of these men began to leave the ranks to defend their homes, which were now threatened by potential reprisals carried out by Union soldiers.

This was the situation of Major Isaac Smith, but his case was more complex than most. He was leaving a new bride in Charleston, along with the rest of his family. They would be safe, however, as his father, Benjamin Smith, was a prominent Unionist who was actively promoting a "New State Movement," which would effectively enable Virginia's western counties to secede from the rest of the state. The elder Smith was becoming an unpopular man with the area's southern sympathizers, and some of this ill will began to carry over to Isaac Smith. Smith faced a problem that was not unlike that faced by many other soldiers from the border states of the Confederacy, but his situation was complicated by the fact that he was an officer and had taken an oath to defend Virginia at a time when his father had openly and visibly decided to support the Union.

Wise and his small army met the reinforcements commanded by Floyd after completing a seventy-mile (113km) march through high mountains over a poor road. Henry Heth, a West Point graduate serving with Floyd (and probably his informal advisor), wrote about the initial meeting that resulted in Floyd's becoming commander of the joint forces due to the fact that he had received his commission prior to Wise. Wise thus became an unwilling subordinate to a rival he would learn to hate. Unfortunately,

William S. Rosecrans turned his army to the south once he was aware that Cox's small Federal army was in a dangerously exposed position at Gauley Bridge. Swift marching by Floyd and Wise could have put the Confederate contingent in position to eliminate Cox's entire force.

many of the men from both factions would suffer as the feuding generals began to hope the other would be defeated by the Union army. Heth wrote of the meeting:

After the usual formalities had been observed, General Wise stood up, placed his hands on the back of his chair and made a speech. I think he spoke for a couple of hours. He reviewed the history of the United States from its discovery, the Revolutionary War, the Mexican War, the causes of the present troubles, his march down the Kanawha River, the affair at Scary Creek, and his retreat to White Sulphur. Floyd listened patiently. General Wise, before taking his seat, asked General Floyd where he was going. Floyd replied, 'Down that road,' pointing to the road on which Wise had retreated. Said Wise, 'What are you going to do, Floyd?' 'Fight,' answered Floyd, intimating that was what Wise had failed to do. If a look could kill, Floyd would have been annihilated, for I never saw greater hatred condensed in a look before or since.

This meeting set the tone for the military relationship between the two former governors, who had taken a political rivalry further than most other people would have considered. Their goals were similar: both hoped to become significant political personalities in the postwar Confederacy.

Wise's tired and poorly supplied troops were ordered to turn around, retrace the route they had taken in their recent retreat, and move into positions from which they could put pressure on Cox's regiments, who had formed a garrison to defend Gauley Bridge, the Union forces' easternmost stronghold. This was the practical limit of the Union army's ability to provide Cox's men with supplies. The need to defend their lines of communication had reduced Cox's numbers and rendered any additional attacks against the Confederates in the nearby mountains unwise.

Floyd's regiments moved to positions upstream from those of Wise and crossed the swift, swirling waters of the Gauley River at Carnifex Ferry, where he would be able to threaten Cox from the north. Cox was in a difficult position at Gauley Bridge: Wise was located just to the east of his positions and Floyd, with a small but unfought army, had moved to threaten him from the north along a good road. The possibility of a combined movement against the small Federal garrison was becoming more likely by the day. Additionally, Floyd's position placed his men in a location from which a swift march across a single ridgeline would place them within marching distance of Charleston, directly on Cox's line of communication and possible retreat. Cox was nearly trapped, and the only potential reinforcements were with McClellan's forces, which were operating along the line of the Baltimore & Ohio. McClellan himself had departed to Washington, D.C., but the able commander William S. Rosecrans had replaced him. Rosecrans made swift arrangements to relieve Cox.

Cox sent the small 7th Ohio Volunteer Infantry Regiment upstream toward Floyd's position to give the impression of an impending attack. The regiment and its commander, however, would be the ones to feel the sting of a surprise attack. The 7th Ohio moved into positions at Cross Lanes, approximately five miles (8km) from Floyd's new "Camp Gauley," where it was surprised by an attack by three of Floyd's infantry regiments, a company of cavalry, and three artillery pieces. Caught during breakfast, the 7th Ohio fought hard against overwhelming numbers. One company was captured by one of Wise's commanders, Colonel Christopher Tompkins of the 22nd Virginia, who shouted "Put down your weapons and you will not be harmed." Others fled the battlefield, and survivors, including Colonel Tyler, arrived at Gauley Bridge telling tales of destruction. It appeared that the entire regiment had ceased to exist, but stragglers kept appearing. Cox and the depressed Tyler were able to recover some optimism when news arrived at their headquarters that four hundred additional survivors under one of the officers, Major Casement, had safely crossed the mountains to enter Charleston and would soon rejoin the command to defend Gauley Bridge from the imminent attack.

Floyd withdrew from the battlefield at Cross Lanes and entered the new fortifications at Camp Gauley, a position from which he vowed that he could resist "the world, the flesh, and the Devil." Unfortunately, the inexperienced Floyd had selected the wrong side of Gauley River to defend against attack, and furthermore seemed to be oblivious to another alarming development: Rosecrans and a large Federal army were on the march from the areas in which they had been operating.

Floyd did not or would not understand how poor the location of the site he had chosen for Camp Gauley was, but Wise knew and did not delay in informing the Confederate War Department of the error made by his rival. Wise had warned Floyd not to cross the river because once under fire, the Confederates would have no opportunity to retreat. Wise wrote: "But cross it he would, and cross it he did!"

Floyd, realizing the possible peril he was in as Rosecrans approached, sent swift messengers to recall Wise's regiments from their positions miles to the southeast. Ordered to march again to support an eastern Virginian general, the men began to grumble as they marched over the same mountain roads for a third time. Thus was the stage set for the Battle of Carnifex Ferry.

chapter 2

CARNIFEX FERRY

The men of Major Isaac N. Smith's regiment, the 22nd Virginia, had just participated in the fighting at Cross Lanes and had been ordered by Floyd to march back to their original command, under Wise. They had no sooner arrived at their destination when they were ordered to return to Floyd. The men in this regiment and the men of the 36th Virginia were nearly all from Virginia's western counties and most had some sort of grievance against eastern Virginia and the politicians there who had been managing the western region of the state as if it were a colony. It was at this point in the Kanawha Valley campaign, on September 15, 1861, that Smith began to prepare a long letter in the form of a diary that he would send to his bride, who was living within Federal territory.

A letter written to my dear wife last Monday gave some particulars about my own movements and those of the army. I propose to write from day to day upon these pages and when an opportunity comes, send them home.

We had just been ordered back to Floyd's camp when I last wrote, after just reaching Wise's camp, and the whole regiment, officers and men, was filled with indignation at the manner in which the poor volunteers were [treated] by the two legions, being ordered to and fro continually.

The commander of the 22nd Virginia, Colonel Christopher Tompkins—a West Point graduate and recent settler into the moun-

"*Every graphic description of this engagement and of Floyd's retreat fell into my hands afterward. It was a journal of the campaign written by Major Isaac Smith of the Twenty-second Virginia Regiment, which he tried to send through our lines to his family.*"

—*Jacob D. Cox*

PAGE 31: Despite enduring many privations, including much terrible weather (as shown here), many Confederate soldiers remained true to the oaths they had taken when mustered into the Rebel army. Unable to return home without breaking those binding oaths, many of these men fought to the end of the war before returning to their homes and seeing their families. ABOVE: Ordnance manuals such as this were quickly adapted and printed in quantity for use by inexperienced Confederate officers.

tains himself—was quick to complain about the treatment of his soldiers. He wrote to Wise on August 19:

Yours of yesterday was duly received. I had received a characteristic letter from Gen. Floyd which has been referred to Genl. Lee. As I am about marching with the remains of these two regiments I have barely time to refer to one or two matters in your letter. You say, 'I hear your men prefer his command. I shall ask him to detach them from mine &

attach them to his.' I do not know who it is that communicates so much camp gossip, nor do I think it worthy of attention.

Nevertheless I protest against these volunteers being transferred like so many coach-horses, & submit that it is entirely unnecessary to request until their preference is ascertained, or even then....

It is telling that Tompkins, a professional officer, was taking the time to lecture his commander, Brigadier General Wise, as he prepared to lead his two undersize regiments to assist Floyd at Camp Gauley as Rosecrans approached. Tompkins apparently had recently received an unkind letter from Floyd and had forwarded it to Robert E. Lee for review. Tompkins, Major Isaac Smith's immediate commander, was not the type of officer who would let his men be misused without a response. He had been sponsored into West Point by John Tyler, recently the vice president of the United States, and he had sufficient political connections in Richmond to avoid any unfair treatment at the hands of either Wise or Floyd. He had corresponded directly with Lee over the "characteristic letter" from Floyd, an indication of the level of support Tompkins had in eastern Virginia. Unfortunately, Isaac Smith had no support from that quarter and with a Unionist father, only the presence of Tompkins insulated him from the wrath of either of the former governors.

The men in the ranks of the 22nd Virginia were also beginning to resent the treatment they were receiving. These were the veterans of the fighting at Barboursville, Scary Creek, Charleston, and Cross Lanes and felt that they had won victories while Floyd had only marched about and made speeches.

Smith continued with his account of recent events on September 15:

Rosecrans was in command of the Union force that attacked Floyd's small army at Camp Gauley, near Carnifex Ferry. Poorly located, Camp Gauley was evacuated in the dark in a high-risk operation before Rosecrans could order a morning attack.

We were told that some 6000 men were approaching to attack Floyd but did not believe it—thought the whole affair was a false alarm. About one o'clock P.M. the regiment was put in motion. We marched about 8 miles [13km] to a camp, about 2 ½ miles [4km] from Carnifex's Ferry in Gauley, near Floyd's camp—next morning moved on, the men ferried over, and hurried up the hill. As we crossed going one way wagons filled with sick, haggard men were being ferried the other. I remained after the regiment had started up to see that our wagon train was started across—had got the first wagon over and then followed the regiment. As I went up the

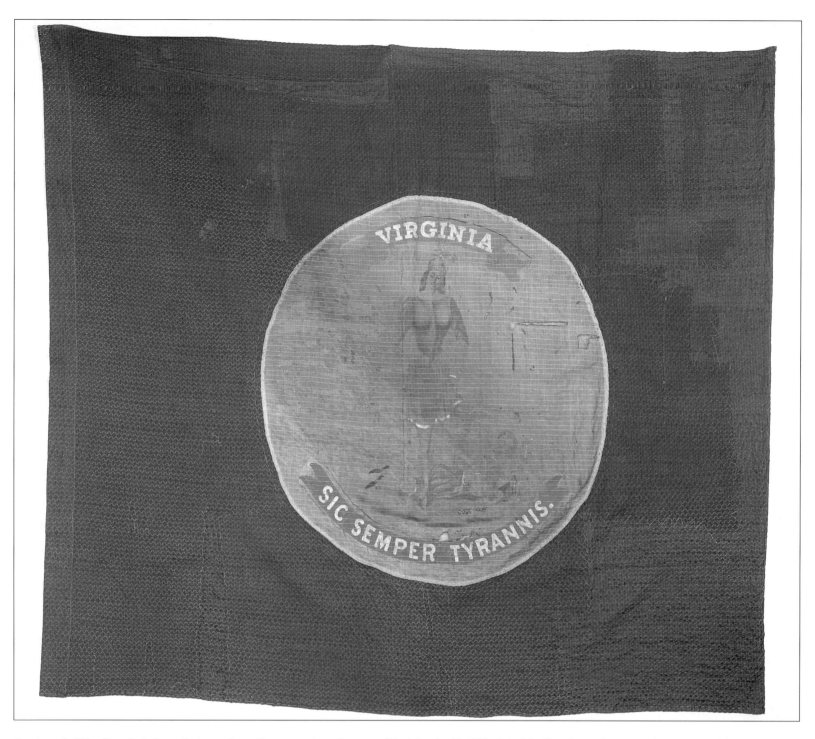

Composed of the fiercely independent men from the mountains of western Virginia, the 22nd Virginia (the flag shown here was the regimental flag of either the 22nd or 23rd Virginia) spent the first three years of the war fighting in the mountains. Emerging into the Virginia area of operations in 1864, these veterans fought at New Market, defended Lynchburg when David Hunter attempted to destroy the city, and were with Jubal Early when he marched on Washington, D.C. The valiant regiment suffered high casualties and lost its commander, George Patton, at Winchester in 1864.

CARNIFEX FERRY

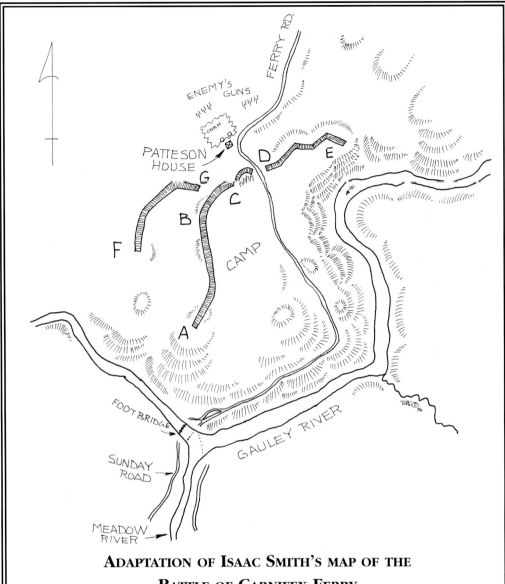

ADAPTATION OF ISAAC SMITH'S MAP OF THE
BATTLE OF CARNIFEX FERRY

Smith illustrated his diary with a rough sketch map of the Confederate defenses at Camp Gauley and provided a legend on the map (see page 10 for original) to explain the position and movements of the 22nd Virginia during the conflict.

AB—Station of 22nd and 36th Virginia Regiments, Virginia Volunteers

BC—Station of 50th Regiment, Floyd Brigade

CD—Battery of four guns

DE—Station of 45th Regiment, Floyd Brigade

FG—Station of 36th and 51st Regiments, Virginia Volunteers (misidentified on original map as elements of the 45th Virginia)

Between lines BC and FG—Three-gun Confederate battery

steep narrow road, it was almost impassable with sick men, fugitive citizens, and wagons and cavalry. I was astonished at the numbers and learned that the pickets had been driven in. The enemy were within a mile [1.6km] of the works. Reached the top of the hill with great difficulty and found the men all drawn up along breastworks, the cannon in position, and the gunners at their posts. The position of our regiment had been defined some time before, and I rode up to it hastily—found them in position, hitched up my horse and took my place in the line.

The worst had happened for the small Confederate army at Floyd's position at Camp Gauley. Wise had previously moved his regiments past the small town of Gauley Bridge, Virginia, as he knew that the Federal troops operating along the Baltimore & Ohio Railroad could march southward over good country roads and get in their rear—effectively trapping them between the Gauley River and Cox's army, which was moving eastward along the Kanawha River.

As noted, the Federal regiments who had gained considerable field experience under George McClellan had come under the command of William S. Rosecrans, another West Point graduate. Learning of the potential trap Cox had entered at Gauley Bridge, with Floyd to the immediate north and Wise's brigade just to the east, Rosecrans moved swiftly to relieve him. Learning from scouts that Floyd's position was nearby and that Wise's force was separate from Floyd's. Rosecrans moved quickly to destroy Camp Gauley. This was the approach of the enemy that had come within a mile [1.6km] and had driven in the pickets in front of Floyd's positions mentioned in Smith's diary entry. Actual combat had not yet begun and Smith described the area:

LEFT: **Confederate Officer,** *by Don Troiani, illustrates the courage of the southern officer corps as they sought to inspire their men to fight bravely against a better equipped and more populous enemy. ABOVE: New River, as seen from Hawks Nest, is much like nearby Gauley River. The swift, tumbling water coursing through dangerous narrow gorges made any thought of impromptu fording impossible; as a result, the few deep pools that accommodated ferries, like Carnifex Ferry, were strategic points for both sides of the conflict in Virginia.*

It was the opinion of nearly all with whom I conversed that the enemy would not dare attack us in our position, but would simply amuse us with a feint, whilst their wagon train passed down the road from Summersville to Gauley Bridge and then would follow the wagons. We had a strong position. I will try to give you some idea of it. Gauley River like New River runs between most pre-

CARNIFEX FERRY

Skirmishing occurred in nearly every Civil War battle as small groups of soldiers attempted to locate the positions of opposing forces, delay an advance of the enemy, or act as an early warning of an attack. The men in this painting by Keith Rocco are advancing to "feel the enemy" and learn of position and intent.

cipitous and lofty mountains with high ranges of cliffs on both sides.

The enemy were cautious in their approach. After waiting some two or three hours, the men hungry and thirsty, Col. Tompkins sent me back to hurry up our wagon, which was the first to reach the ferry.

In order to reach the road from our station (near to A), it was necessary to ride along the lines and to close to them until the road was reached, then go down the road. I had just got to the first gun at C when I saw one of the men start up saying 'there they are!' and looking over the breastworks (for on horseback I was high above them) I saw one-two-three men coming—just at the edge of the forest. The General ordered the men not to fire without orders.

These three Federal soldiers who produced such an alarm within the Confederate fortifications were skirmishers who were leading Rosecrans' initial brigade toward combat. Rosecrans made a personal reconnaissance of the potential battlefield and ordered his lead brigade commander, Brigadier General H.W. Benham, to move forward. These men had been marching since four o'clock that morning, for nearly twelve hours, and were very tired as they moved forward.

An experienced engineer officer, Benham was also a West Point graduate and had served in the prewar National Army. As he had no engineer on his brigade staff, he scouted forward. Benham later wrote:

I kept with the head of the regiment to avoid ambuscades, and to judge myself of their position and arrangements. After advancing about one-fourth of a mile [402m] to the end of the woods, I halted the command, and could perceive that a heavy crossfire had been prepared for us at the open space at the debouch from the roads.

Within five minutes of this time, (nearly half-past three o'clock) while carefully examining their earthworks on the road in front and their entrenchments on our left, a tremendous fire of musketry was opened on us, which in a few minutes was followed by a discharge of grape and spelter canister from a battery of some six pieces of artillery. This caused a break in the line for a few minutes, though for a few minutes only, for the men immediately returned to their ranks, under the lead of their officers, to their former position, where I retained them as I was certain that the fire at us through the close woods was without direct aim, and because they were needed for the protection of the artillery, which I immediately ordered up...throwing shells well into their intrenchments on our left.

Isaac Smith and his regiment were the recipients of much of the return fire from Benham. Of the fusillade Smith wrote:

I, of course, started back to my regiment in haste, the firing began at once. The line AB is not visible from the forest. We had to cut it out of the thickest brush I ever saw, but observe its position and you will see that the enemy's guns were so placed as to rake the line from one end to the other. Their position was higher than line CD, the enemy directed

their fire at the guns mostly, and as they always shot too high, the cannon balls, shell, etc., all came up along our line and rather low, too. There was scarcely a gun fired by them which did not send its rifle cannon balls, grape canister or fragment of shells among us. We could not see the enemy nor could they see us, but we expected after each fire a ball among us. We could not tell the explosion of our guns from theirs and could see neither.

Federal Brigadier General Benham continued to describe the fighting as it developed:

After passing through the woods for a half a mile [804m], our skirmishers were suddenly engaged in front, and I pushed on to their relief until I reached a cleared space on the summit of a hill, where, for the first time, the enemy came into view, posted in force behind an extensive earthwork with twelve guns in position to sweep the road for over a mile [1.6km]. A ravine separated the hill, by which we approached from the right of the breastworks of the enemy, which was composed of logs and fence rails, and extended for over a mile to the right and left of their entrenchments, affording secure protection to their infantry and riflemen.

Confederate Drummer, by Don Troiani. At the onset of the Civil War, the use of the drum to coordinate troop movements was associated with the infantry on both sides of the conflict, while the bugle was widely recognized to be the mode of communication of the cavalry. The benefits of using a bugle were soon recognized, however: a bugler could carry a firearm and move about freely, while a drummer could carry no weapons and was hampered by the heavy drum.

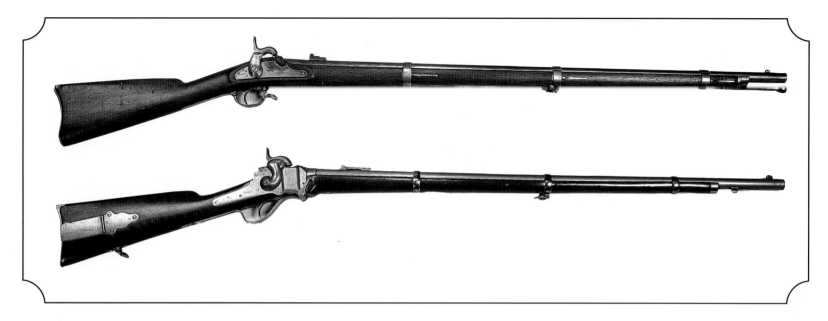

Civil War weapons included the 1861 Springfield (top) and Model 1859 Sharps rifles. Both were used by the soldiers on either side during the Civil War.

When the head of my column reached a point opposite the right centre of their earthwork, their entire battery opened on us with grape and canister, with almost paralyzing effect, my men falling around me in great numbers.

The Battle of Carnifex Ferry had opened in earnest as Union regiments closed with the Confederates, who were sheltered behind strong earthworks. Whitelaw Reid, a reporter from a Cincinnati newspaper who was traveling with the Ohio regiments, wrote:

Skirmishers found themselves about two hundred and fifty or three hundred yards [229 or 274m] in front of some sort of fortification; exactly what, it was impossible to see. The enemy seemed to discover them about the same time. For a few moments there was a resumption of the sharp but scattered firing, then suddenly there came a terrific clash of musketry, and a perfect storm of lead. The enemy had opened along his whole front....

The heavy volume of musket fire and cannon blasts from the Confederate breastworks against the Federal troops in the open was thought by both sides to have produced a "fearful slaughter," but the terrain and thick vegetation gave some protection to the attacking Federal soldiers. Fortunately for the Confederates, their earthworks provided both concealment and cover from the return fire.

Isaac Smith continued his account of the battle in his diary:

The enemy attacked each line separately and late in the evening, we supposed, got around our line. We have reason to believe that what we supposed was the enemy was our scouts. The scouts were certainly there, and received a heavy fire from us. When our fire opened, the enemy, who had almost ceased firing, opened upon us, and some of our own guns were directed to that part of the ground so as to help us, but our men had the benefit of both fires as we were not in sight of either battery. This

affair ended the engagement which had continued about three hours, sometimes very active, at others desultory and almost without the report of a single gun.

The officers and soldiers during the early Civil War lacked both skill and experience and such mistakes were common on the battlefield. Isaac Smith described how his regiment had accidentally fired into a group of scouts, but there was another command error in this battle. An "extemporized" Federal brigade had formed to assault the Confederate right side and the men lost their way in the darkness. The Union commander reported:

Col. Moore reported that it would take until two o'clock in the morning to get two companies of his regiment up. I then ordered the whole column to "Face About!" and march out just as it had marched in, and crossed the ravine to the rear of the column to lead it out,

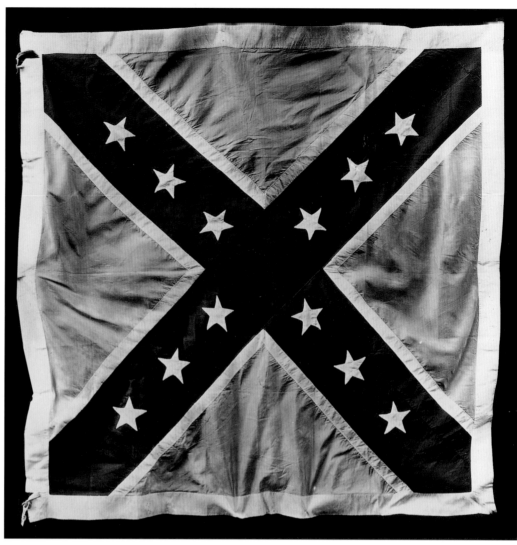

LEFT: This painting, **Rebel Yell**, *by Don Troiani, captures the excitement among the brave men of the Confederate army as the war cry commonly heard before an attack on Union positions went up. In this depiction, a Confederate regiment has broken through the opposing force's line and is in the process of capturing a Federal battery. ABOVE: The square battle flag of the 13th Virginia Infantry Regiment was similar to many of the Confederate regimental flags carried in the war.*

when a shot or two from the enemy's skirmishers, or an accidental shot from one of our own pieces, caused the whole column, doubled as it was into a "U" shape, to open fire, killing two, and wounding about thirty of our own men.

The reduced visibility and the near exhaustion of the Union soldiers brought the

CARNIFEX FERRY

While dramatic, this depiction of the Battle of Carnifex Ferry by German soldier J. Nep Roessler, showing Rosecrans' troops attacking Floyd's fortifications at Camp Gauley, is historically inaccurate. While the Union had several killed and wounded men, the Confederates had only a single man wounded in the conflict—General John B. Floyd.

This photograph of the cliffs at Gauley Bridge shows the rugged terrain in the area over which the soldiers of both sides had to maneuver. The fallen trees in the foreground are the remains of obstructions scattered by Union troops across the roads to protect Cox's positions as he was set upon by Floyd.

Sixteen-year-old Confederate soldier Maxmilian Cabañas was typical of the boys who rushed into the service on both sides of the Civil War. This young man was later to die in a Federal prison.

fighting to a halt as darkness fell. The Union regiments remained close to the Confederate positions with the obvious intention of continuing their attack the following morning. Isaac Smith described the results of the afternoon's combat in his diary:

> The breast-work, except in front of the artillery, was very incomplete, made of rails and brush, and on our line afforded no protection as the enemy's fire came in behind us or along the line. John Thompson, son of Dr. Thompson of Putnam and acting adjutant of our Reg't, was wounded almost in the beginning of the fight by a ball shot at our gunners from a point near the house. It is about ¾ of a mile [1.2km] from the house to the place at which Thompson stood.

No one else was hurt in our regiment, no one was killed, and I believe but four wounded on our side, none mortally. Two of those terrible rifle-cannon balls passed nearly the whole length of our line, just high enough to have knocked the heads off the whole line of men—one ball went about 10 feet [3m] in rear. The last passed just over Plus' back as he threw himself on the ground and about three feet [91cm] from Col. T. Plus acted as aid to the Col. during the engagement and was constantly with him as he was walking up and down the line. A ball passed just over the head of all three of us while at my end of the line (the rightwing half of the regiment) discussing the progress of the fight. A piece of bomb shell fell between Wm. Reynolds knees as he was sitting on the ground, he sat still and dug it out of the ground where it buried itself.

A canister or piece of shell fell just before me a few feet and buried itself in the ground so deep that I could not dig it out with my sword.

The fighting at Carnifex Ferry would have been far bloodier if the participants had been more experienced at the time of the battle. Participants described the Confederate fire as the heaviest ever heard, and one two-gun section from the Union army fired ninety rounds from positions that were approximately four hundred yards (366m) from an opposing Confederate battery. It is unlikely that the

Confederate officers and enlisted soldiers were often depicted in brave, patriotic poses in the media and in propaganda to inspire support among the southern population. Because the Confederacy was essentially under attack from "northern invaders," the defenders of the South's territory and institutions assumed heroic proportions to the civilian population early on in the conflict.

CARNIFEX FERRY

Union artillerymen would have survived well-aimed counter-battery fire.

General Floyd was holding very strong positions, but in the rear of the Confederate positions were terrain features that would complicate any attempt to retreat—especially if the Confederates were under fire as they attempted to evacuate. The area was described by a newspaper reporter from New York:

The rear is protected by gigantic cliffs, shooting up in perpendicular line three hundred and fifty feet [107m] above the river, and where there are no cliffs the surface of the mountain, except on two narrow lines which lead to the ferry, are so steep and rugged that an armed man could not scale them if opposed with a broomstick....Gauley River, a wild, roaring, beautiful torrent, also covers the rear perfectly. The rapids are dangerous above and below, but at the ferry the stream is wide and very deep.

Under the circumstances, a retreat under fire from a determined enemy was a military impossibility, teaching Floyd and his senior staff another lesson in the military arts. Floyd, a skillful politician, had placed his defensive positions on the wrong side of the river and had those high cliffs and a raging river directly to his rear. If a man armed with a broomstick could prevent an enemy from escaping, a trained Union infantry brigade on the high cliffs would be capable of decimating any of Floyd's retreating soldiers caught in the act of evacuating their fortifications. Timing would be critical to the success of any planned evacuation from Camp Gauley.

Isaac Smith continued to describe events in his diary:

I have no idea what effect our fire had upon the enemy—some think it very

This Confederate jacket is typical of the locally manufactured items used by the southern army. Chronic shortages of basic necessities caused by a limited manufacturing capability and the Federal blockade forced Confederate soldiers to make do with equipment that varied widely in appearance and quality.

President Buchanan's cabinet had to deal with significant domestic political problems, including John Brown's attack at Harpers Ferry and South Carolina's attack on Fort Sumter. The cabinet members are (left to right): Jacob Thompson, Lewis Cass, John B. Floyd, President Buchanan, Howell Cobb, Isaac Toucey, Joseph Holt, and Jeremiah Black.

Confederate artillery was drawn by cattle (as opposed to horses) in the early stages of the war as the resource-poor Confederacy attempted to counter-maneuver against Federal forces.

fatal. I do not. I believe we made no great impression on them. At any rate night only stopped the engagement and the enemy evidently held their ground for the purpose of renewing the attack next morning. The men were kept to their places behind the breastwork—had nothing to eat, but little water since early that morning with the certainty of a severe battle the next day. Our wagons had been ordered back to re-cross the ferry. We sent men down to bring up something to eat and all the axes that we might strengthen our breastwork which was extremely weak and afforded little or no protection. About 10 o'clock a message came for Col T and myself to come to headquarters. On our way we met Mike coming with food for us—sent him on to wait our return. At headquarters found Genl Floyd's tent filled with officers. He was wounded slightly in the arm and had it bandaged in a sling. Everything was stiller and more solemn than a funeral. Genl Floyd then told Col T that from good sources he had learned that Genl Rosecrans with nine regiments had formed the attacking party and that without additions to our small force of about 1800 men we could not whip them and that a retreat had been determined on by the officers and asked his opinion.

Defeat at the hands of fellow West Point alumnus William S. Rosecrans, who had led the successful operations along the Baltimore & Ohio Railroad, was a distinct possibility that had to be taken into consideration by the ambitious John Floyd, since capture by Federal forces would prove exceptionally embarrassing for the Confederate.

Earlier in his career, southern sympathizer Floyd had abused his position of power as the secretary of war in the Buchanan Administration to transfer small arms to armories in the South. He had also made an attempt to transfer 124 cannons from Pittsburgh to posts in the South, where these heavy weapons would fall into the hands of the nascent Confederacy. In addition to these questionable activities, Floyd had also been implicated in an attempt to sell the Fort Snelling reservation to a New York syndicate and had been accused of the misuse of $870,000 in Indian Trust Bonds. He was saved from possible arrest and prosecution by a disagreement within the Cabinet over possible courses of action in response to the attack on Fort Sumter. This provided a convenient excuse for Floyd's resignation and return to the newly secessionist state of Virginia. Floyd was certain that Federal courts would revisit several outstanding indictments if he ever fell into the hands of the Union army.

Confederate Study, by Keith Rocco, reveals a poorly equipped infantryman. Cast in the role of the defender of home and community, and often asked to perform miracles on the battlefield, the Confederacy's soldiers became legendary for the valor they displayed during the Civil War. In spite of equipment shortages, poor food, and extended absences from home and family, these men frequently won battles against heavy odds.

Smith continued to describe the preparations for the Confederate retreat:

The retreat was then ordered and as usual it was decided that our regiment should bring up the rear. In a retreat this is the most dangerous service, as the rear guard must keep everything before them, wagons, cannon and everything, and are held responsible for the safety of the whole train. Floyd sent his own regiments first—McCausland (who is a sort of favorite) next and ours last. We had no wagons of our own to guard. They are all over the river and had been ordered away by Col T but we had to wait until everybody else got off before we could move. It was also necessary that everything should get over the river before daylight, and without the knowledge of the enemy for after we left the top of the hill, a few hundred men could station themselves on the cliffs and shoot us down like dogs—either with cannons or small arms. Our regiment did not move until about 12 o'clock. Col T and I expected most certainly to be taken prisoners with the whole regt, knowing it would be almost impossible to cross before day. I forgot to mention that during the day a foot-bridge had been finished across the river, by which the soldiers could cross but wagons and horses had to take two little flatboats which could ferry one wagon at a time.

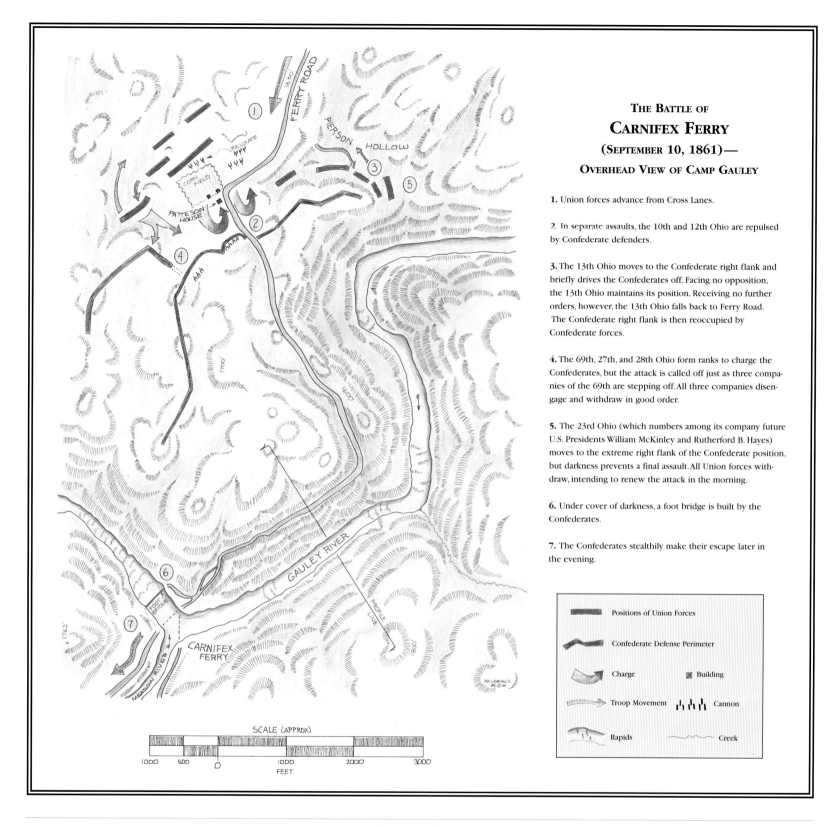

THE BATTLE OF
CARNIFEX FERRY
(SEPTEMBER 10, 1861)—
OVERHEAD VIEW OF CAMP GAULEY

1. Union forces advance from Cross Lanes.

2. In separate assaults, the 10th and 12th Ohio are repulsed by Confederate defenders.

3. The 13th Ohio moves to the Confederate right flank and briefly drives the Confederates off. Facing no opposition, the 13th Ohio maintains its position. Receiving no further orders, however, the 13th Ohio falls back to Ferry Road. The Confederate right flank is then reoccupied by Confederate forces.

4. The 69th, 27th, and 28th Ohio form ranks to charge the Confederates, but the attack is called off just as three companies of the 69th are stepping off. All three companies disengage and withdraw in good order.

5. The 23rd Ohio (which numbers among its company future U.S. Presidents William McKinley and Rutherford B. Hayes) moves to the extreme right flank of the Confederate position, but darkness prevents a final assault. All Union forces withdraw, intending to renew the attack in the morning.

6. Under cover of darkness, a foot bridge is built by the Confederates.

7. The Confederates stealthily make their escape later in the evening.

SCALE (APPROX)

1000   500   0   1000   2000   3000
FEET

Positions of Union Forces

Confederate Defense Perimeter

Charge   Building

Troop Movement   Cannon

Rapids   Creek

Confederate Standard Bearer, by Don Troiani. The man who carried the battle flag, his regiment's symbol, became a target to opponents, who hoped to break the fighting spirit of the regiment by capturing his flag as a trophy. The capture of a Confederate flag normally resulted in a medal of honor for the captor; not surprisingly, standard bearers were frequently killed.

Virginia as they performed their rear guard duties during that terrible night. Fortunately, the influence of Tompkins and Smith must have had a steadying effect on their men, who were caught in this terrible position due to the bumbling of the inexperienced Floyd.

Isaac Smith requested permission to check on the cause of the delay in getting the artillerymen into motion:

I proposed to go up and see what was the matter to which the Col gave a hearty assent. Went up—found some of the men lying on the ground, the horses not harnessed to the guns, and many of them without harness on—the baggage lying about in every direction—the Capt not on the ground—called for an officer. After some time found a lieutenant sitting on a stump drumming his heels against it. Remonstrated with him—told him I believed his guns were lost unless the movement was made immediately and that his caissons would almost certainly be lost—explained the danger he was in of losing everything and our connection with it. The men seemed perfectly astounded, seemed to know nothing of what was going on, and as I have learned says they had no orders to move. Went back and reported these facts after taking the authority to order the guns off immediately. Col T sent me back to repeat the order in his name also— found the Capt this time. The men were in great confusion. I went to each gun, hurried up the men (none of the guns were limbered) and staid there until I saw them all start off. All of this of course occupied more precious time before daylight. Again set out down the road to the ferry, stopping every moment or two on account of the crowded condition of the road before us. The wagons, guns, caissons, etc., made it almost impassable even to those who had a right to go forward.

Incredibly, Floyd and his staff had been in such a rush to cross the river that they had forgotten to give the evacuation orders to their artillerymen. Smith, Tompkins, and the soldiers of the 22nd Virginia who formed the rear guard could not join the retreat until everyone else had left the camp, so this neglected order had threatened their safety as well. One young private, Thomas J. Riddle, who served in the artillery that night, wrote that "many of us were asleep behind our breastworks when the evacuation was ordered...and nothing disturbed our slumber save some groans of the wounded, not far from our fortifications, until an officer of the guard awoke us, saying that we had orders to evacuate our position as soon as possible." Smith's alertness had saved them from certain capture when daylight revealed the Confederate retreat to Rosecrans' nearby sentries. Smith continued to describe the retreat in his diary:

The road down to the ferry is steep and worse than any road you have ever traveled on Poca and just wide enough to admit a single wagon. It is precipitous above and below, and down in between two high mountains in the dense shade the darkness was most intense, it was impossible to see anything. From our start after the artillery until we reached the river is about one mile [1.6km], perhaps not more than ¾ mile [1.2km]—we were at least two hours on the march. You can imagine the suspense during its slow progress. In order to find a place to sit, we passed the wagons and guns and reached the banks of the river. The 36th Regt passed on over the bridge. Gauley River is like New River in its character at

Jacob D. Cox was the commander of the Federal garrison at Gauley Bridge that joined in the pursuit of the small Confederate army commanded by Floyd and Wise as the Rebel forces retreated from Carnifex Ferry.

this place; Meadow River empties into it and there is smooth, but swift water for about two hundred yards [183m]. Above and below there are rapids and falls—the falls are about ½ mile [804m] long, full of tremendous rocks. There is no escape for the unfortunate man who should be drawn into them. The frail and narrow bridge was about 50 or 75 yards [46 or 69m] above, the water running swiftly under it. A few dim lights were burning along the bridge—there was no railing. Some four or five poor fellows fell over—I heard some were drowned but believe they were rescued.

Most of the small army had managed to cross Gauley River on the improvised bridge that was completed the day before. Unfortunately, Smith, Tompkins, and their men had to remain in their current positions. Floyd had ordered them to be the rear guard of the army and they had to stay on the shore opposite the route to safety.

Isaac Smith further explained their situation to his wife in the diary he was keeping for her:

We, of course, remained—Col T more and more impressed with the danger of losing the whole force by capture and seeing plainly that the ferry could be defended so much better from the other side and with only the ordinary dangers of the battlefield, crossed and mentioned his views to Genl Floyd, who co-incided with him and ordered us across. It was beginning to clear up for daylight, and you can imagine the gratification of the men when they discovered that they were not to be sacrificed but to fight on fair terms. I started them over the bridge single file about five feet [1.5m] apart. In about half an hour the whole force had crossed, and after calling out again and

again along the shore to see that none were left. Plus (who had stood at the end of the bridge with a light to see that the men went single file and at proper distance) and I walked over arm in arm, the last of the 22nd Regt and of the forces (except for some artillerists) to

cross. I have never experienced relief so great as when I set my foot on shore on this side, knowing that my whole regiment was safely across, not one lost or injured. From a seeming certainty that all would be lost, suddenly all were found safe. The crossing soon progressed

The Confederate cavalryman (seen here in a depiction by A. Tholey) was the elite soldier of the first half of the Civil War. Born into a society in which horsemanship was highly valued, the men and boys of the southern cavalry generally outrode and outfought their northern horse-riding cousins. This would change dramatically in 1864 and 1865 as Federal cavalrymen improved their skills.

so far as that Genl Floyd ordered us to leave a ferry guard of one company to remain and destroy bridge and boats when all were over and march on. On top of the hill we stopped for about an hour when the men took a little something to eat. Here I found Mike who had arrived with the horses just a short time before us, having been since 8 o'clock the night before in going about two miles [3km]. The delay was at the ferry, of course. I was determined if the Yanks took me they should not get my new cavalry saddle I had purchased two days before.

Smith, Colonel Tompkins, and the men of the 22nd Virginia were finally safe. They had formed the expendable rear guard of Floyd's army and all of them might have been sacrificed because of Floyd's ignorance of military tactics and subsequent blunders. It was fortunate for the men that Rosecrans' initial attack failed to break through, or all of them would have been effectively taken out of the war as either casualties or prisoners.

Once he had reached the relative safety of the next mountain range and new defensive positions, Smith wrote of the narrow escape he and his command had experienced:

I have never felt anxiety such as was experienced that night. The safety of the whole regiment was involved and the honor of its officers and of the service depended on the issue of that movement. If we were even successful in getting everything across, we would be so long delayed as to make a fight or surrender inevitable—to fight down in that ravine would have been almost madness—to surrender would have laid us open to reproach, no matter what might have been the circumstances. Floyd does not

Accessories, such as this belt buckle and buttons, were hard to come by in the Confederate army. The belt buckle in particular was rare; the eleven stars around the initials probably represented the western states of the Confederacy at the time the buckle was made.

like Col T because he knows that Col T despises his character as a man and has no respect for his qualifications as a soldier and it would suit Floyd's view to leave Tompkins to bear all the blame which might attach to any mishap in the retreat.

Southern newspapers reported Floyd's hastily and inefficiently managed retreat in the most glowing terms. One reporter wrote, "I think that the public and all military men will agree that our fight and our fall back to the other side of the river are among the most remarkable incidents in the history of war." No one stopped to question the military reasoning that placed the small Confederate army in such a vulnerable position in the first place. Instead, newspapers carried such lines as "I think these facts show a generalship seldom exhibited anywhere" in overly generous praise of Floyd, whose

hopes for a prominent role in the postwar Confederacy must have therefore been lifted considerably.

The battle was over and both sides began to claim victory, but this is more accurately described as a stalemate in which both sides won something. Rosecrans was able to force Floyd to retreat from positions from which they were threatening to engulf the outnumbered Federal garrison under the command of Brigadier General Jacob D. Cox at the small but strategic hamlet of Gauley Bridge. The Confederate army survived as an intact military force and was able to withdraw into the mountainous terrain eastward along the James River and Kanawha Turnpike. They moved into defensive positions past a vital road junction where a road from Summersville entered the turnpike, a route that would have permitted Union forces to get at the Confederate rear if the Rebels had been stopped at earlier positions.

chapter 3

SEWELL MOUNTAIN

Major Smith continued to write in his diary about the Confederate retreat over the Gauley River:

> We marched to a place on the turnpike about two miles [3km] above Vaughan's, but as we were in the rear of everything, the march was provokingly slow. We were all day making 8 miles [13km]. Camped here and remained until Thursday night—were ordered to march from there at about 10:30 P.M. Marched all night—the men were terribly fatigued with loss of sleep. Stopped about 1½ miles [2.5km] below Frank Tyree's at about 10 in the morning of Friday. Remained here all day and night. Next morning (Saturday) moved on to the top of Big Sewell. Remained here Sunday and Monday—the men were engaged in fortifying. Monday night 10 o'clock again ordered off. Just as we got the men formed a terrible rain came upon us, the poor fellows had to stand and take it without shelter or motion for about two hours waiting for the slow regts who were to move before us to get off, and when we did start, the men were marching in mud over shoe tops, the rain drenching them beside.
>
> Whilst we were drawn up waiting, the quick report of three guns in the direction of our pickets was heard and presently the cavalry picket of three or four near camp came dashing in, saying the advanced guard of the enemy

PAGE 57: About General Robert E. Lee, Smith had the following to say: "[He] was known to be the most talented man in the U.S. Army after Genl Scott—is about 6 feet [183cm] high, a most perfect figure, straight without stiffness, full chest, trim built in every respect, decidedly the handsomest figure I ever saw...." Even this paragon would age dramatically due to the stress of the Civil War. ABOVE: Whether Union or Confederate, Civil War soldiers frequently took advantage of a new innovation, the camera, to preserve the memory of their participation in this sweeping conflict. As a result, the Civil War is one of the earliest wars to be so richly documented with photographic images.

was approaching within a mile [1.6km], and they had fired into it. This was startling news indeed and I believe I came nearer being scared than at any time since the war began. Everything was in such utter confusion, part of the force gone, and the other part just leaving, and the 22nd Regt occupying a position which would force them to engage the enemy first, and so situated that the enemy would be entirely protected by the woods whilst we should be in open ground. I thought we stood a poor chance, but I got all right pretty soon and after a great deal of alarm and apprehension all around it was discovered that the cavalry dragoon had fired upon our own infantry picket which

This portrayal of soldiers in a rainstorm in Virginia's western mountains shows the great hardships suffered by both sides while maneuvering during the 1861 Kanawha Valley campaigns. Severe weather conditions, including extensive floods, effectively halted preparations for a major battle between Lee and Rosecrans in the Sewell Mountain area in the fall of 1861.

had been stationed beyond and were returning to camp to join in the march.

This march was decidedly terrible. Mud, rain, cold, hunger, and loss of sleep combining to make it as uncomfortable as possible. You will observe that in one week we march three nights. If the march could begin and then the men go on until they came to a stopping place it would not be so hard, but each regiment and its wagons have their place in line, and must not pass it, so that the toiling up hill of heavily loaded wagons keeps the men constantly on the move, but never stopping for any length of time. One stalled wagon stops everything behind it. Each regiment follows its own wagons. We marched to Meadow Bluff, where the Blue Sulphur Road turns off. The object of coming here is to prevent our rear being reached by the road from Nicholas Court House which also comes here. The men had scarcely prepared for bed last night, hungry and tired, when another order came for another forced march to begin at 3 o'clock next morning and for four days rations to be cooked. The poor fellows of course would have to cook all night before the march and thus get no sleep at all. Fortunately, however, an order came first to postpone time of march to 5 o'clock and afterward countermanding it altogether, for good reasons.

I might say much about these matters but it would be neither prudent or proper.

Floyd's inability to manage his small army and the incompetence that resulted in the misuse of the Confederate volunteers from Virginia's western counties had begun to have an impact on Major Smith. He and the other volunteers were present in the

Confederate camps such as this were not always available to the men of western Virginia's regiments. Officers may have been able to afford wagons in which to transport their personal belongings and tents in which to shield themselves from the elements, but the enlisted men were often forced to sleep in the open or in improvised shelters called "brush camps."

ranks because they had elected to defend their homes from what they presumed would be an invasion of angry northerners. They were willing to risk their lives in the service of their state, but were quickly learning that their efforts were not being recognized by their commander; as a result, many men

began to have second thoughts. Smith, many of the other soldiers, and the commander of the 22nd Virginia, Colonel Tompkins, had begun to have serious doubts about their continued service under Floyd, whose poor leadership continued to expose the rear guard to danger—from Federal bullets to

pneumonia—while Floyd's favorites traveled in relative safety and comfort at the front of the army.

In addition to his other problems, Smith was about to lose the services of Mike. Mike, often mentioned in Isaac Smith's diary, was the young officer's personal slave and served both Smith and Tompkins. Smith wrote of the loss:

Mike, after many expressions of faith-lessness, etc., left our wagon on the march from Dogwood Gap last Thursday night and has not returned. He sent me word that he was sick and had to stop but took good pains to keep out of my way, although he knew that I was behind at the head of the column. He had a wagon to ride in and many a poor sick fellow I saw dragging himself along that day who had no other way to come. Col Tompkins' brother-in-law saw him marching back down the road toward and near the enemy and turned him back. Genl Wise did the same and put him in charge of a soldier to bring back but the fellow escaped him. Dr. Wilkins told him to go to the hospital which was near and he would give him medicine and a good wagon to carry him on. The sickness was all false, but he was making it for the Yankees. Look out for lies from him. He will use every means to run his wife and children off, and will doubtless be aided by the Yankees. You know he is liable to confiscation by their law, as he has been actually used in the service. Watch out for the rascal and believe none of his excuses for leaving.

Isaac Smith had been accustomed to slavery—the "peculiar institution"—all of his life. As a moderately well-to-do southerner, he had been raised in a society that owned slaves. Now that he had lost one he wanted "it" back, just as he would have attempted to recover any other expensive piece of personal property that was lost. At this point in the Civil War, the Emancipation Proclamation had not been signed and senior Federal officers were returning escaped slaves to their own-

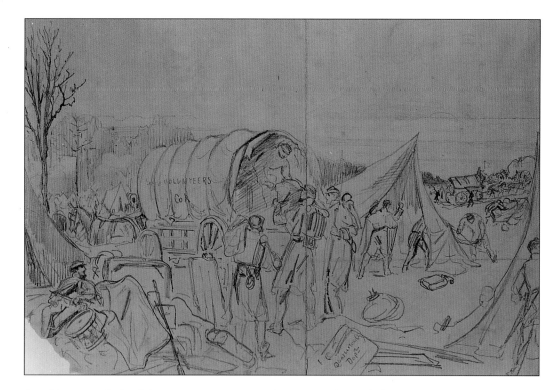

Breaking camp in the Union army was more complex than in the Confederate army. Supplies from prewar national army stock were readily available initially, and later on contracts were made with northern industrialists to fully equip the growing Federal forces. Tents and wagons were in abundant supply by the time the Union regiments began to campaign in the mountains. It was only after Gauley Bridge was reached that their supply lines became overextended.

ers rather than alienate slave-owners in the crucial border regions.

Smith's father, Benjamin Smith, was a staunch Unionist who was heavily involved in the "New State Movement" that would eventually be successful in the creation of another Union state, West Virginia, from Virginia's western counties. Curiously, the elder Smith was the actual owner of Mike and soon appeared at the Federal camp at Gauley Bridge to reclaim his missing "property" from General Jacob Cox, the area commander. Cox wrote:

A negro man was brought to my camp by my advance guard as we were following Floyd to Sewell Mountain in September. He was the body-servant of Major Smith, and had deserted the Major with the intention of getting back to his family in Charleston. In our camp he soon learned that he was free, under the Act of Congress, and he remained with us, the servants about headquarters giving him food. When I returned to Gauley Bridge, Mr. Smith appeared and demanded the return of the man to him, claiming him to be his slave. He, however, admitted that he had been servant to Major Smith in the rebel army with his consent. The man refused to go with him, and I refused to use compulsion, informing Mr. Smith that the Act of Congress made him free. The claimant then went to General Rosecrans, and I was surprised by the receipt, shortly after of a note, from headquarters directing the giving up of the man. On my stating the facts the matter was dropped, and I heard no more of it for a month, the man meanwhile disappearing.

Up to this point in the diary, Major Smith had been explaining events that had transpired in the recent past. He began daily entries as events occurred, beginning on September 18, 1861:

Since Thompson was wounded it has been the duty of Sergeant-Major (Plus) to act as adjutant and he has done well. He has called forth praise from Col Tompkins for his promptness, which is itself a volume of commendation, for he seldom praises anything in these rabble hosts as he regards all militia.

I have written this for the family generally, thinking the narrative would be gratifying. Read it to them. I have expressed opinions somewhat too freely for a junior officer, but am speaking to those whom I know will not permit me to be made instrumental in damaging the service. Such things, of course, should not be generally discussed lest they might get to Yankee ears.

The Union army did, however, get an opportunity to learn of the views held by the younger Smith. The communication was captured with other letters being forwarded through a complex delivery system called "Dixie Mail" into territory occupied by Federal units. The diary was probably read carefully by Federal officers and then passed to Benjamin Smith, a man with whom General Cox had become friends. Cox understood the complexity of the local situation in Virginia and wrote that "Even the leaders of the Unionists found their own 'house divided against itself,' for scarce one of them but had a son in Wise's Legion and the Twenty-second Virginia Regiment was largely composed of the young men of Charleston and the vicinity."

In many ways Virginia, with its eastern and western factions, was a microcosm of the entire Civil War. Accordingly, many families were split between the Federal and Confederate armies, with fathers and sons fighting in opposing camps; numerous were the mothers and wives who prayed that their

"Writing Home," one in a series of newspaper illustrations called War Scenes About Washington, *shows a young drummer boy writing a letter. Isaac Smith was typical of a large number of Civil War soldiers in that he was literate; separated from their families and living in adverse conditions, many of these men and boys wrote many letters to their loved ones. Interestingly, the surge in writing led to the mass production of lead pencils to meet the demand during this period.*

This is a photograph of the first entry in Smith's diary/letter to his wife, dated September 15, 1861: "A letter to my dear wife...." The diary became a fascinating account of much of the early fighting in western Virginia, the arrival of Robert E. Lee in the area for the first time, and the rivalry between Floyd and Wise that contributed to the loss of the region to the Union. Smith's conflicting loyalties—to his regiment, to the region of his upbringing, and to his Unionist father—resulted in some of the more poignant surviving diary entries from the Civil War.

closest family members would never meet in battle. Loyal regiments were raised in areas that contributed equal numbers of young men for service in both armies. This was a difficult time for all involved and the hard feelings that arose in this area during the Civil War remained for generations afterward.

Major Isaac Smith wrote faithfully into his diary from that point onward. Perhaps the notes he wrote for his wife—who might one day read them after he was already dead—made him feel closer to her as she stayed at home in Union-controlled territory. Regardless of motivation, Smith turned out to be an excellent reporter of events as they developed around him. He wrote on September 19, 1861:

A pleasant day yesterday, no exciting news or rash orders. This morning came news that the enemy were marching rapidly upon Wise, that Wise was determined not to retreat, but to await their attack. Our whole force was therefore ordered out to prepare for the attack upon our lines, and have been actively engaged in throwing up breastworks all day. We are fortifying the east bank of Meadow River on both sides of the turnpike just this side of Little Sewell Mountain. The lines are about three miles [5km] long. Our left has about 400 yards [366m] on the left flank, where a road comes in from the Wilderness Road. The boys worked well to-day although they have only about 10 axes. Every other regiment was supplied with quite a number of shovels, picks and axes. Our point is one of great importance, and especially so under the news that the enemy were advancing in force along the road from Nicholas CH, an outlet of which we are to defend. If they have no artillery we can whip them—

with artillery they will hurt us considerably as the hills on the other side of Otter Creek completely command our position. The place we occupy is condemned by every Col in the forces I

As in any war, propaganda was used by both sides in the Civil War. Patriotic scenes such as this one were designed to inspire high levels of civilian support during the war. The South, defending itself from an invasion from the North, had a distinct advantage in rallying support on the home front: many northerners were opposed to the continuation of the war, and there was a serious concern in 1864 that the peace candidate, ex–Union general George McClellan, would be able to defeat Lincoln.

believe—it is a selection of General Floyd's.

I must go to bed for there is every probability there will be commotion tonight, perhaps some movement. It is very certain we will hear Wise's guns tomorrow—and we may probably fight ourselves. May God preserve us all. In Him is my trust.

Here was the first indication of a subtle change in the outlook of Major Smith. He had written of danger and hardship associated with military service, but he had continued to perform his duties without complaining. He had been an officer in the Confederate army for only a few months, but he was beginning to recognize the problems that he would continue to encounter. Chief among his problems revolved the incompetence of John B. Floyd. Smith had experienced a retreat from the Kanawha Valley (his home), a small victory at the battle of Cross Lanes, and a poorly planned retreat from miserable positions at Carnifex Ferry across Sewell Mountain, and was now being assigned to defend the most likely point to be attacked by numerically superior Union forces. He had a total lack of faith in the ability of General Floyd to lead his soldiers to safety—much less a victory—and this belief was shared by Colonel Tompkins as well as most of the men of the 22nd Virginia.

The misuse of the 22nd Virginia, combined with the stress of the campaign and a retreat from the homes the men had sworn to defend, had begun to erode the morale of Smith and many of the soldiers under his command. It is at this time that Isaac Smith invokes the Almighty for the first time in his diary. The combination of poor leadership, bad food, superior enemy forces, and homesickness had begun to have a palpable impact on Isaac Smith and the soldiers of the 22nd Virginia Infantry Regiment.

Smith was unable to write in his diary for the next three days, but brought his account of the campaign up to date with an entry on September 22, 1861:

Contrary to expectations no fight yet. Wise has not even engaged the enemy although 12 miles [19km] in our front. We have had a more quiet time than usual. No orders at night—everything regular and quiet as though we were 100 miles [161km] from the enemy. Everyone is more or less surprised at their inaction—can't understand why they don't attack us or try to outflank us and get in our rear.

Genl Lee of the Northwest army and Commander of the forces in Virginia arrived at our camp last night. This morning the field and staff officers and Captains of our regiment called upon him in a body to pay our respects. He was known to be the most talented man in the U.S. Army after Genl Scott—is about 6 feet [183cm] high, a most perfect figure, straight without stiffness, full chest, trim built in every respect, decidedly the handsomest figure I ever saw— his features equally handsome, and his face and eyes are full of intelligence— courteous and perfectly easy in his manners, and with the most remarkable faculty of keeping his own counsel I have ever known—perfectly circumspect

OPPOSITE: In General Robert E. Lee, Don Troiani has captured the regal bearing and natural leadership of the great southern general. His appearance regularly left observers awestruck, a fact that is reflected by the hyperbole in much of the writing about him. Major Robert Stiles, who met Lee during the Peninsula campaign, wrote of the encounter: "A magnificent staff approached from the direction of Richmond, and riding at its head, superbly mounted, a born king among men."

SEWELL MOUNTAIN

65

in all he says, answers all questions civilly, but with good care that no one shall find out more than he intends them to know. One thing is certain that not the least symptom of the politician appears in his manners or conversation but on the contrary everything that characterizes a gentleman. We shall all feel every confidence in his opinions and directions, and the whole army will act willingly upon his suggestions. We are not advised what his course will be, whether he will remain here or return immediately to his command. It is probable he will straighten up matters here, set these two political generals on the right course in the right way and then leave us.

West Virginia Homeguards were assembled from local Union supporters and were armed by Union authorities. Incited to punish secessionist neighbors for their support of the Confederacy, their raids and burnings provoked reprisal attacks from Confederate Partisan Ranger units and contributed to the development of hard feelings among neighbors that lasted for generations in the mountain clans.

Smith and the men of the western army had high hopes in the person of Robert E. Lee. Here was an answer to their prayers: a trained, experienced general who was viewed as the best soldier in the entire country had come to review the actions of the untrained former governors of Virginia who had been appointed brigadier generals, John B. Floyd and Henry A. Wise. These two generals had been feuding since they both arrived in the western theater of operations and were carrying their political rivalry into their military activities. Each would have preferred to see his rival defeated by Rosecrans than to have been able to win a major victory for the Confederacy west of the Allegheny Mountains. Unfortunately for the men who were serving in the ranks who had homes and families living in areas now falling under Union control, Floyd and Wise were rapidly losing the Kanawha Valley and western Virginia to the invading Federal army. These soldiers had entered Virginia's service in order to defend their homes and families, but the army was being withdrawn to positions from which they could defend eastern Virginia. Word began to be passed around campfires in the evening that "West Virginia has been sold out" and desertions began among the enlisted men as several officers resigned their commissions.

Unfortunately for Major Smith, events were beginning to transpire that would severely test his loyalty to the Confederate army. He had learned from a friend that his father, an unshaken Unionist, had become an object of hatred as well as a target for possible attack. Smith wrote:

I am much depressed today from various causes. This unhappy war is growing more and more fierce every day, and there is less prospect of peace than ever. Vile passions are aroused and terrible scenes yet to be enacted. West Virginia is to be red with blood before the end—yet my source of constant trouble is that my father will be in danger. Wicked and unscrupulous men with whom he has lived in friendship for years absolutely thirst for his blood, as I truly believe. He and Summers, as one of their friends remarked to me today, are especial objects of hatred and aversion to men here. I am actually leading a set of men one of whose avowed objects is the arrest and judicial or lynch murder of my father. The situation is a terrible one and I cannot continue in it. Much as I regret the differences of views which we may hold, yet it is not proper for me to be so situated. My father has been neutral and committed no act which would subject him to imputation but in this war, prejudice and passion decide everything on both sides; reason and facts none.

Isaac Smith and his father, Benjamin, may have had different opinions on the politics surrounding the Civil War, but the elder Smith was a civilian who was not ordinarily subject to the rules of war as long as he did not bear arms. Unfortunately, emotions—"vile passions"—were clearly aroused and the population's belief and contentions began to harden as casualty lists on both sides began to lengthen. The Civil War in the mountains of Virginia was becoming a bitter, serious family feud fought out among different households, and the Smith family was to be no exception.

Isaac Smith had a cousin, Joab Smith, serving as a private in the 22nd Virginia. Joab, an educated man who had been a schoolteacher prior to the war, wrote about his uncle Benjamin as his regiment retreated through Charleston: "I saw that notorious traitor and cold-blooded villain who seemed to delight at our misfortune. In fact, the hoary-headed scoundrel could not conceal his

This is a photograph of page 16 of the Smith diary: "I am much depressed today from various causes...." It was written as Smith began to realize that the war would be longer than anyone had previously thought. "Vile passions" were developing as casualty lists grew on either side, placing his father in danger from his fellow Confederates. Smith began to question his own position and wrote on seeing the national flag, "in spite of my position I love it yet." He felt that it was a strange and unnatural war.

delight. Great God! To think that I should be related to this infernal demon in human form!"

Isaac Smith was correct in his assessment of the situation facing his father if Smith the elder should ever fall into the hands of the Confederate soldiers of his son's regiment. If the nephew could feel such a degree of hatred toward his uncle, Benjamin Smith could expect little mercy from strangers in the ranks. There is little wonder that Major Smith felt depressed as he contemplated his probable future. He completed the diary entry for the day, perhaps the low point in his military service:

> *This is Sunday—no preaching, no service, no godly conversations, no Christian considerations are a part of the day's duties. Our chaplain has never been near us since we left White Sulphur and only there for a few days. Everybody is intent upon the shedding of blood, upon war and its evils, upon the follies of earth and not upon the love, the mercy and goodness of God.*
>
> *I am in no humor to write—the future is terrible. I have no control over my own fate—if free from the army could not visit my friends or even hear from them; have no conception from day to day where the morrow will find me or even the next hours—and the future of my life (if God's mercy gives me length of days here on earth) how utterly darkened inscrutable—I can have no plan.*

The hope generated by the arrival of Lee at the mountain encampment was outweighed by the information Smith received about the developing hatred directed at his father. His grief was of the sort commonly felt through western Virginia at this time as young men found themselves torn

Confederate officers were usually drawn from the pool of aristocratic young southern men, many educated in southern military academies. Used to riding and hunting from an early age, these men had a distinct advantage over their less experienced northern opponents during the early stages of the war.

by conflicting duties to regiments, loyal friends, political preferences, and families. Nonetheless, many of them were able to continue to serve within their regiments until the end of the war, and fought until the end of the hostilities finally came. This was an especially cruel war.

Events began to transpire along the lines of confrontation that kept Smith from making any additional entries into his diary until the following Sunday, September 29. Wise had refused to move from his positions on Sewell Mountain in open defiance of General Floyd's orders. Lee had returned to the area, inspected both locations where the feuding commanders had constructed fortifications, and urged Wise and Floyd to unite to face the oncoming onslaught of Rosecrans' large Federal army. Lee directed that the two small armies join forces on Sewell Mountain; Major Smith provided details of the encampment in his next extensive diary entry. He had recovered from the depression he had shown on the previous Sunday:

How remarkable that we are here. What is written above shows my ignorance of what was to happen. On Monday night (23rd) received orders to have tents, baggage, and everything packed in wagons, one day's rations in haversacks, and every man and company ready to start at 5 o'clock next morning—got the men ready by the time fixed but had no orders to move. Waited longer, had the men formed and waiting, in about two hours or more received orders to march—our regiment in advance, and then ascertained for the first time that Genl Wise was about to be attacked at Big Sewell, and we were to go to his relief. You will notice that our regiment usually is put in front on an advance and in the rear in a retreat.

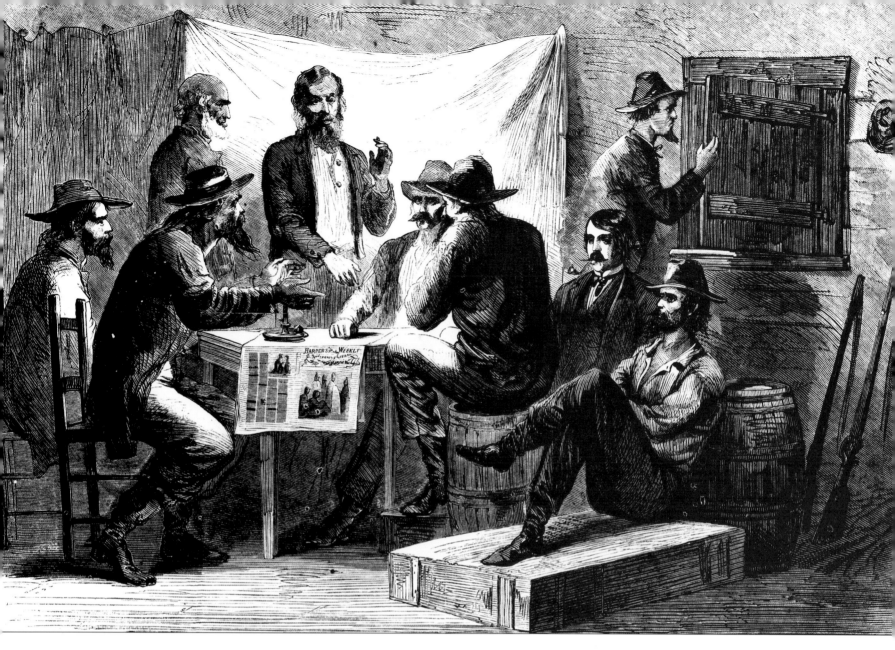

Secret meetings of southern Unionists (such as Isaac Smith's father) occurred frequently in the mountainous regions of western Virginia, where sufficient support was developed to create a new state, West Virginia, in 1863. Similar groups of Unionists were formed in western North Carolina and eastern Tennessee, where the mountainous terrain had limited the use of slaves and reduced any sympathy for that institution. Secret associations like the Red Thread and White Thread Societies and the Heroes of America encouraged draft resistance and desertion from the Confederate army.

Moved the regiment and went about 100 yards [91m], and found the wagons were not to go. Col Tompkins had two biscuit in his haversack—was sent back by him for a canteen, and took occasion also to get three biscuit with a small piece of meat in each in my hurry. This was the only stock for Col T. and myself. Marched rapidly, met men and wagons from Wise's camp at almost every turn. Many of the men had great stories to tell of how pickets were shot, etc., etc. The wagons were hurrying to the rear and we met some going rearward very rapidly whom we thought should be going forward.

At the top of Sewell or near it (Mrs. Buckingham's old place) halted for a moment to rest the men, had scarcely sat down when the booming of a cannon was heard. The Col jumped to his feet, called out 'Forward' and we were off again.

It was about 2 or 3 o'clock when we reached the first troops. We were marched off into the woods and shown our place along the top of the ridge, no breastworks or defenses had been made. The men were deployed behind logs, trees, or in open ground along the line and stood awaiting the attack. Continual firing among the pickets was heard—one poor lieutenant carried along dying in a litter, shot at the outpost—every gun created the impression the enemy was upon us. The men moved to their posts and with hand upon the locks of their guns watched for the enemy to show himself before them—we were in the woods where the enemy had even chances with us.

On the way down Col T and I had together eaten one biscuit—late in the evening I ate another. Neither water or food except that, from 3 o'clock in the morning—the evening wore away and no attack. The men had set to work, one half watching, the other working, with about four axes had managed to do something towards a breastwork. Many of the poor fellows had nothing to eat all day. They had relied upon the wagons and had started out on the march when the wagons were ordered back. Guard out all night. Slept on a few leaves with Col T, in the middle of the ridge road, just behind our lines—troops and horses were passing at all times during the night within 2 or 3 feet [61 or 91cm] of us.

Up at four o'clock—almost certain of attack—had the men all along the lines. Same expectation and anxiety and watchfulness of day before, jumping to the guns and breastworks at every gunshot. The men worked hard and by night had made an excellent line of breast-

works fully protecting the whole line of some 3 or 4 hundred yards [274 or 366m]. Still nothing to eat. Some time in the forenoon Gen Wise sent some flour and beef—men were sent to cook. They used the barrel heads to cook upon, and about night some warm dough and some beef burned upon the coals were distributed—no salt either in the bread or on the meat. A piece of bread about the size of one's hand and a small piece of meat were given to each man. Some received none until after night. This was the meal of the second day. 3rd day (Thursday) about the same scenes, food of the same character but a little more of it. I cut my dough into thin slices, browned it thoroughly and ate it with water—could eat no more beef. In the afternoon it was evident rain was coming on. We got some of the men to build us a brush camp—the rain sprang up

before it was finished, and in a short time it was saturated and came pouring through as badly as there was no shelter. In a short time we were saturated. Tried to sleep but could not—water almost running under us, and a leak dropping in my face, and many others running upon my body. At about midnight all gave up. Plus tried to sleep and probably did; after 12 the balance of us sat up—the dough was thoroughly saturated by morning—took it wet upon a chip cooked it once more.

This was the remains of the night before, when we had some bread with salt in it, and some potatoes (quite a feast). The rain poured on pitilessly; the poor fellows were shivering in the wet and cold—the blankets of many were in the wagons at Meadow Bluff. All day it poured on. A more merciless, cheerless rain, and more miserable day could

Confederate headgear came in a wide variety of shapes, and several different examples could usually be seen within a single unit. The kepi, an example of which is shown here, was one of the most prevalent types.

Sewell Mountain's rugged beauty and terrible weather are depicted in this sketch by the 47th Ohio's J. Nep Roessler. Here, a Federal scouting party conducts a reconnaissance of nearby Confederate positions at Wise's Camp Defiance. Poor weather, disease in both camps, and destruction of the ferry at Gauley Bridge by flood waters stopped preparations for a major battle.

SEWELL MOUNTAIN

It was not uncommon for Confederate soldiers to desert their regiment and turn themselves over to the Union army during the 1861 campaigns. Usually recruited to defend their homes in western Virginia, these young men lost their reason to fight once the Confederates surrendered the region to Union forces and retreated to the east, leaving their loved ones behind. Major Smith's wife and family had remained in Charleston when the Union army occupied it.

scarcely have been experienced by any-one. The poor, half-frozen, half-starved men had to stand it. We were all thoroughly drenched and with difficulty kept the rain from extinguishing our fire. Some of the men seeing our destitute condition came and offered to build us a slab camp. Just after this, to the joy of all, some of the wagons came in, bringing tents and provisions for the boys. Our wagon came along, our tent was pitched, and in a short while we had a nice supper of excellent hot coffee, good bread and butter, and cold turkey and ham. We enjoyed it, of course. This is Sunday and this morning it was reported that the enemy had made a movement, and an attack was expected,

SEWELL MOUNTAIN

and everybody put on the alert. I have been writing here, expecting at any moment to hear the guns. This morning we felt almost confident of attack, and every falling tree (the men were strengthening the breastworks) made us start.

A great deal of activity had transpired in the week since Smith had mentioned his depression. General Floyd's regiments had been marching rapidly back along the James River and Kanawha Turnpike, a trip they had just completed in the other direction, to reinforce General Wise's positions on Sewell Mountain. The formidable combined armies of General Rosecrans and General Cox had moved along parallel courses after the battle at Carnifex Ferry. They had shown that they were willing to fight aggressively as they moved their brigades across mountainous terrain in the West to attack Wise's small army at Camp Defiance.

Wise had had enough of the overbearing John B. Floyd and refused to retreat any farther with him. He halted his small brigade on Sewell Mountain and began to correspond with Lee, in northwestern Virginia, and complained about his dual problems: Floyd and the peril he faced from the Union army.

It was at this point in the Civil War that Robert E. Lee's hair began to turn gray. Floyd wrote to him that Wise refused to obey orders to reunite their separated brigades to face Rosecrans' attack together and Lee was soon forced to move his headquarters to the vicinity of Sewell Mountain in an attempt to manage the two feuding Confederate generals. Shortly after he arrived at Floyd's camp, he wrote to Wise, "I beg, therefore, if not too late, that the troops be united, and that we conquer or die together."

Wise responded with a letter claiming that his positions were the strongest of the two and that Floyd was in total error in posi-

tioning his brigade at Meadow Bluff in order to prevent a swift march by Rosecrans from the vicinity of Carnifex Ferry to gain positions in his rear. Floyd was preoccupied with his fear of capture; Wise knew the precise positions of both Rosecrans and Cox, who were marching directly to Wise's position to eliminate his brigade before moving forward to destroy Floyd.

Wise agreed to join forces under Lee after informing his commander that "perhaps he would soon be the subordinate of no living man"; Lee agreed that Wise had occupied the best position from which to engage Rosecrans, and he ordered Floyd's brigade to march to the west to relieve Wise. Lee was in charge of the entire expedition.

On the brink of battle with Union forces, Isaac Smith continued to describe the military situation in his diary:

There are two tops to Sewell Mt, one about a mile [1.6km] from the other, the enemy are camped on the western, we on the eastern—the enemy are camped where I wrote the first part of these pages. From many places in our line, we can see their whole camp—large number of tents, all over the hilltop, and men walking about among them. Last night we heard the band playing with great distinctness—the bugle playing 'tattoo' and 'extinguish light' signals. It seems so singular that we should be here so near and for so deadly a purpose. I feel much more like taking them by the hand, urging them to let us alone, to go home, end this fratricidal war and whilst they live under their government, to let us live under ours unmolested.

The trip, as you may see, has been one of great hardship. General Wise's folly has occasioned it—he refused to obey Floyd's orders, and go back with him to Meadow Bluff, and the conse-

quence is the enemy found him here— he was not able to withstand them and had to send for reinforcements. This Friday the poor old man had orders from Jeff Davis to report to Richmond immediately and turn over his command to Floyd. Nothing could be more humiliating—he despises Floyd, and now while all of his ambitious hopes have been ruined, he goes back to Richmond in disgrace, and his old enemy takes his command.

Wise had no intention of leaving his brigade as his men prepared for battle with a superior force. But when he was advised by Lee to "obey the President," Wise left immediately for Richmond.

Henry Heth, then serving as a colonel in Floyd's brigade, wrote about the meeting between Davis and Wise: "Mr. Davis said, I presume in a playful way, 'General Wise, I think I will have to shoot you.' General Wise started from his seat and said, 'Mr. President, shoot me. That is all right, but for God's sake let me see you hang that damned rascal Floyd first.'" Wise was transferred to command defenses on the Outer Banks of North Carolina and was soon fighting for his life against Ambrose Burnside's amphibious invasion. The colorful and outspoken old man survived and was with Lee at Appomattox.

At one time, Wise had been cautioned by Lee about his profanity, in response to which Wise is reported to have said, "General Lee, you certainly play Washington to perfection, and your whole life is a reproach to me. Now, I am perfectly willing that Jackson and yourself shall do the praying for the whole of the Army of Northern Virginia, but in Heaven's name, let me do the cussin' for one small brigade." It was no wonder that Lee's hair turned gray in the mountains of western Virginia during 1861.

The Confederate soldiers serving in the mountains were glad to have Lee as their commander. They had seen enough of the antics of Floyd and Wise, whom they no doubt felt were responsible for the loss of their homes and families to the Union invaders. Smith wrote:

Gen'l Lee is in command here, and the troops have every confidence in him. Our position is remarkable—I believe if we could go back with honor, we should do so, but the Gen'l cannot turn while thus face to face with the enemy, and we believe the enemy are in precisely the same situation. We can get no provisions here—the bridges along the meadows have been washed away, and the road overflown—wagons cannot get along. Our last barrel of flour goes today not ours but the troops of the 22nd Regt. The poor horses are starving. In two days mine had had six ears of corn and a small armful of hay. Chestnut leaves is all they get. The woods of course will be wretched after this rain, even when the water recedes. We could get the food if it could be hauled.

I have but little hope (indeed none) that the troops will reach the Kanawha this Fall—(I must go for some horse feed somewhere). May God preserve you all.

I am writing in the slab camp, Plus is smoking—Dr. McDonald reading my bible. We have just had a good dinner— ham and potatoes—remains of turkey, bread and butter, and good molasses.

The Confederate infantry corporal was pre- pared and equipped like most of the other men in his regiment. He carried a blanket over his shoulder, a tin or wooden canteen, a tin cup, and a haversack that contained (usually very scant) rations. Many of these men subsisted on corn— both green and dried—that was scavenged from local farmers' fields.

SEWELL MOUNTAIN

Slept better in this camp last night than at any time since leaving home. At night it is impossible to realize that I am in ⅜ mile [1.2km] of an enemy who may kill me in a few moments—feel and seem to miss Uncle Brad.

This is a strange and unnatural war.

This difficult and dangerous campaign, being conducted to defend the homes of eastern Virginians as the western Virginians lost everything to Union occupiers, was rendered even more miserable by extremely poor weather conditions. The mountainous region where the two armies were preparing to fight one another was experiencing one of the worst rainstorms in known history. Mountain roads and bridges were washed out and both armies were running out of food. Diseases, such as measles and pneumonia, were beginning to break out among the unprotected troops living in the open. Floyd later reported: "It cost us more men, sick and dead, than the battle of Manassas."

Both of these armies had stretched their supply lines to their limits as torrential rain hampered the efforts of quartermasters to get supplies forward from depots in the rear to soldiers in the field. Ice had formed on nearby Valley Mountain during the night of August 14 and the heavy rains had raised both New River and Kanawha River past flood levels.

The Union army's supply lines moved through a bottleneck in the region at Gauley Bridge, where a destroyed bridge had been replaced by a temporary ferry. The few supplies getting across the ferry would vanish rapidly if the ferry became inoperable due to the high water. This would leave Rosecrans' army in an untenable position—trapped between a raging river in their rear and Robert E. Lee and a numerically superior army in their front. William S. Rosecrans was too able a commander to overlook this as a

potential outcome and made suitable reparations for an emergency maneuver, if it became necessary.

In the midst of these horrendous conditions, Smith continued with his diary on September 30, 1861:

A few moments after I ceased writing on yesterday, learned that Col Spaulding had just been killed by the enemy's pickets. He commanded one of Wise's regiments. Has been intoxicated for several days and on yesterday, ordered out one of his companies and started for the enemy—went some distance beyond our lines, met the pickets, turned his Co

back and rode up to within a short distance of the pickets—three of whom fired at him, killing him almost instantly—his horse wheeled and ran back to the Co and he fell into the arms of his men. The whole thing was unauthorized and of no use but very sad.

I am officer of the day today and as such it is my duty to visit all of the guards. I have looked forward to it with some apprehension as at one of the pickets a number of men have been shot by the enemy and at another several of our own men have been shot by our own guards, when they were going to relieve or visit the sentinels. This morning went

Thanks to mass production, eating utensils were readily available in the Federal army. In fact, some soldiers were able to purchase this gear from sutlers who accompanied the soldiers into their camps as a sort of traveling PX.

to the advanced picket (that which is nearest to the enemy's line) and was shown where one of our own men had been shot by the enemy—expected every movement to draw their fire as we (the officer and I) were in full view and good range. The officer informed me that I was the first officer of the day who had visited that advanced guard, much less the advance sentinel. Because from this point there is a fine view of the enemy's camp because so near—can see men and horses plainly and the 'Star Spangled Banner' (in spite of my position I love it yet) waving in the breeze—will have to visit the guard again tonight after 12 o'clock. This is one of the regulations of war. Don't fear anything from the enemy on this visit but have much to fear from the guard itself.

One regiment have shot two lieutenants and one man in a week of their own body, at the same post.

Isaac Smith was a complex individual who had stronger ties to the state in which he lived than to the national or separatist government. Unlike many of the relatively uneducated men who served in either army, Smith was a college graduate, an attorney who had served as a state representative, and a man who mixed freely with the socially prominent people who managed the affairs of the region. In spite of the fact that he had taken an oath as an officer in the Confederate army, he still retained a strong attachment for the national flag and the many things it symbolized. This was a difficult time for many of the young volunteers, who had become separated from the families they had sworn to defend. Loneliness, despair, and some level of fear brought them together to seek comfort in religious activities on this particular weekend. In summing up the entry for September 30, Smith wrote:

Last night Frank Noyes, Dave Ruffner, Donaldson, J. Doddridge, Alline Brown and others came to our camp and we sang a number of excellent hymns, had one prayer book and nothing else for words; it was a decidedly pleasing way of winding up the Sabbath, illy as it had been spent.

It is thought probable by some that we shall fight within a day or two—we will probably attack them if they do not attack us. I was told so today but not upon decided authority. If we attack it

General Robert E. Lee, with Custis Lee (left) and Walter Taylor (right), shows the results of the four years of Civil War combat. In only a short time, Lee had gone from "the handsomest figure I ever saw..." (according to Isaac Smith) to an exhausted elderly man. The "strange and unnatural war" had a tremendous impact on most of its participants, in particular its leaders— Abraham Lincoln also aged perceptibly during that time.

will be with great loss of life—for the enemy are strongly entrenched. Something will surely have to be done for we have a large force here now and reinforcements coming every day.

Lee and Rosecrans had settled into a waiting game as each of the contending generals hoped the other would launch an attack into opposing defensive positions where the defender would be able to inflict massive casualties. Lee had received an additional nine thousand men from his northwest command by the end of September and his reputation in the prewar army was sufficient to make Rosecrans cautious. Neither general was prepared to risk the huge losses that would have resulted from an attack.

While awaiting the order to attack or defend against an attack, Major Smith found time to make another diary entry on the following day, October 1, 1861:

Visited the outposts of our line of sentinels last night. Plus said he would go with me to be on hand if anything occurred and at one o'clock we set out. There were such a number of outposts that it would take three days to visit all so I suggested to Genl Lee that I should only visit those next to the enemy which he approved, the others being of less importance we were out about 2½ hours, much less than I expected. Nothing unusual occurred and today I was relieved at 8 o'clock A.M. Will not have to go on duty again for a long time as there are so many officers here now.

There are many indications of early action here. Genl Floyd has moved with his troops making a movement to the rear and I am much afraid we shall be ordered to join him. When we fight again I wish it to be under Genl Lee not a politician.

Jefferson Davis and his cabinet sit with General Lee in the Council Chamber at Richmond. President Davis is seated at the table to the left of Lee, who is pointing to a map.

Smith's entries reveal two interesting factors at this point in the conflict on Sewell Mountain. Apparently there were so many poorly qualified officers in the western portion of the Confederate army at the time that Lee himself was involved in managing the activities of the officers of the day. Normally, an army will have several competent officers on the staff who will develop rosters and assign administrative duties such as this, but in this case, Lee made the decision to modify standing orders for the officers of the day. Second, it reinforces the impression that the soldiers held their political appointee general in contempt; what's more, they probably feared that their lives would be squandered uselessly under Floyd's lamentable stewardship.

Echoing the thoughts of countless combat soldiers before and since who write to loved ones whom they fear they will never see again—frequently, letters and diary entries such as these are meant to be a farewell from beyond the grave—Smith completed the October 1 diary entry on a more personal note:

Wm. H. Ruffner came into camp today from Rockingham, bringing bedding, lint bandages for sick or wounded— hear from him that Miss Julia has reached Ashland.

Jim Lewis stayed here all day yesterday and last night trying to get a discharge from the service—a violent 'secesh'—and it is so with many others

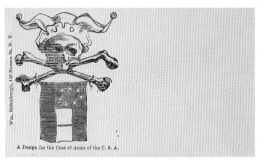

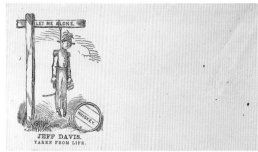

Patriotic (and in this case inflammatory) stationery was used by the soldiers on both sides when they wrote to their loved ones at home. Confederate President Jefferson Davis was commonly the target of northern cartoonists; in fact, the noose was sometimes referred to as the "Jefferson Davis necktie."

of that ilk who hang around the army and run to the rear when there is a fight. By the way, when Plus and I got back last night, found Lewis on my bed tick with his shoes on and all my covering and Plus' on him. He paid no attention to either of us, but slept on. Plus and I were cold and sleepy, and I got no more rest. At 4:30 had to get up and warm and have not lain down since. Col Tompkins from this and some other little matters took a violent dislike to him.

Rain again today—waked up by it at 4 o'clock this morning—continued all day—dull and dispiriting. It is probable that the meadows will again be overflown, and we shall be troubled about provisions. I cannot see how we shall fight here to any purpose if half starved. Under the circumstances we could not pursue the enemy if we ever defeated him. Deserters (I hear) have come into camp saying they were famished in their camp.

I am afraid continually that I shall never see the loved ones at home again. If we attack the enemy there will be terrible slaughter—why should I again survive when so many are certain to be lost. It is my great trouble when about to go

into action that my separation from all was so unexpected. How little we thought when I left the house Monday morning that it was to be our last meeting for a long time, and very possibly forever. I dread an action on this account than any other. Floyd's troops have joined us here. Our large force cannot long remain inactive.

Smith didn't have an opportunity to write in his diary for a few days, but on October 5 he continued to document the situation on Sewell Mountain:

Yesterday and the evening before was a busy and exciting period. We had received intimations that the enemy would attack the following morning (yesterday). I was greatly depressed for I am afraid of never meeting you all again, but was active and ready to do my duty as I believe hitherto on such occasions I have faithfully performed. The battle when it comes, will be severe, and hotly contested. I feel pretty confident of the issue being favorable to us. We can hardly be whipped here. At quarter past three o'clock we were all up, and ready shortly after to receive the enemy. Every moment we awaited the

opening of the enemy's guns, and so continued until late in the day. At 12 o'clock I thought it no more than probable no attack would be made during the day. You have no idea of the excitement such a state of things produces, but I have been so long accustomed to such things that the effect is nothing like it would be to the inexperienced person. We looked for the enemy today but not so much as yesterday. A prisoner taken today says the enemy have 24,000 men and more on the march, and will attack when their forces arrive.

We have been told that Mr. Quarrier has been arrested and sent to Columbus. I have never believed it; heard of Major Parks' and Goshorn's arrest, and today that Goshorn had been returned. Did not believe this, until informed they were sent to Wheeling not Columbus. The Major had Cox's safe-conduct and guarantee but the most outrageous baseness would permit it to be violated.

The war was beginning to take a savage turn. In the above entry Smith was expressing his concerns about the safety of his wife's father, Mr. Quarrier, one of Charleston's most prominent citizens. The series of arrests began when General Wise ordered the imprisonment of a prominent Unionist, Colonel Thomas A. Roberts, a member of the Second Wheeling Convention that attempted to form a new Union state from Virginia's western counties. In retaliation, one of the first acts of the Union army when it occupied Charleston was to order the arrest of Major Andrew Parks, a former state senator, as a hostage to guarantee the safety of Parks. Smith may have been able to put the arrest of Parks into a better perspective if he had known of the nonjudicial arrest of Roberts at the order of General

Wise. Unfortunately, such arrests and counter-arrests would soon become commonplace.

Isaac Smith wrote of a family friend, Creed Parks, who—like many other soldiers at Sewell Mountain and in the Civil War in general—had fallen ill:

Creed Parks has stood the whole campaign like a brave fellow as he is, until a few days since, when he has been obliged to go to Meadow Bluff on account of sickness. I think the hardship and exposure just after we came here has occasioned his illness. Tell Cousin Margaret that as soon as I learned of his illness, I did what I could for his comfort. Yesterday he was sent back, out of harm's way in case of an engagement, and where he could receive better attention and food, and is of course beyond my aid. If he gets worse, he will be sent to Lewisburg to the hospitals established there. Creed will probably get into some house and will be well attended at Meadow Bluff. Looking every moment for the enemy yesterday, I could not go to see him before he left, but was told he had a place to go, to which he could go. Creed was threatened with fever, and was not seriously sick when he left, but may be so hereafter. He was growing better when sent away and may recover at once.

These two armies suffer terribly here when Sewell begins to show itself in its true light. At present the weather is delightful.

Tomorrow is the Sabbath again. I lose all account of the week days about the middle of the week, but hunt up the day (by comparison with others) towards the end so as to know the Sabbath. We shall have no service unless Mr. Ruffner will come up and preach for us. He is on

Confederate pickets stood guard at lonely outposts between the lines (as in this painting, Confederate Pickets in the Snow, by Don Troiani), both to provide early warning of attacks and to deter enemy patrols. Poorly equipped, these men suffered terribly due to the elements, and many died from disease. For instance, many of the soldiers who caught measles while living in rustic camps frequently died from complications related to the virus.

Meetings between Rebel and Union pickets were common occurrences between actual battles. The former countrymen exchanged news from home and frequently traded between themselves. Confederates provided tobacco and Federal pickets provided coffee.

Little Sewell awaiting a battle and will be here to aid in taking care of the wounded. O how I long to spend one more Sabbath at home—to hear the old familiar church bell, to meet my old friends in God's house in preparation for the duties of the day—to sing the songs of praise with old familiar voices and faces, to hear my own kind pastor from our own sacred desk—to enjoy the calm tranquillity of a home Sabbath. Indeed to meet once more the loved ones at home and with them once more endeavor to devote to God the holy day he has set apart for his worship.

I have just finished making a haversack—cut it out, sewed it entirely myself and it is a good effort. Made it out of a

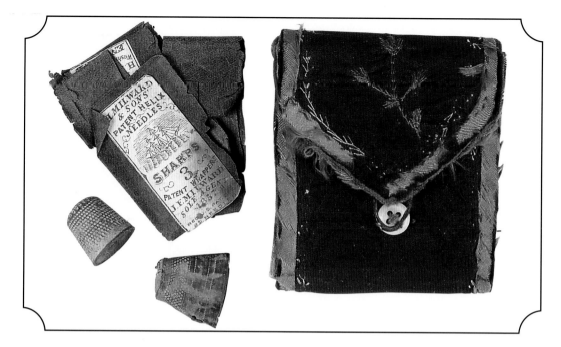

The "soldier's housewife" was a small sewing kit that was carried to make timely repairs to clothing and equipment. Isaac Smith used a similar sewing kit to construct a haversack, an accomplishment that he proudly reported in his diary.

piece of torn linen. Am delighted with my success in this new business.

Have just learned of an opportunity to send this and will now write a short letter to Callie with it. The opportunity comes at exactly the right time as the paper has given out.

Smith ran out of paper at this point, but anyway was unable to send the diary home when he had hoped. The opportunity had passed, and he kept the diary with him. He returned to making entries on October 16, almost two weeks later, from a location far removed from the anticipated action at Sewell Mountain:

When I last wrote my paper was used up. I believe the same evening I wrote the last sheet I was perfectly astounded to receive an order detailing me as Officer of the Day to fill up Col Read's

tour who had gotten into some trouble and had to be taken off duty. This was the second time in one week, when I had supposed I should not be called upon for nearly a month. At one o'clock that night I set out alone to visit the pickets, mad and lonely, and found that one of the pickets, Capt John Quarrier's Co now commanded by Lieut Ray (Quarrier sick and gone to Richmond) had heard great rumblings of wagons, etc. and had reported it. The other pickets had heard wagons but thought there was nothing unusual as they had heard them nearly every night. Went to all the pickets near the enemy and consulted the officers, none of them thought anything of the matter but Ray, and Ray thought no great deal of it. I thought of going at once to report at headquarters, but concluded to consult Col Tompkins who thought it best to...do nothing about

it. I left orders with the picket to send me a messenger immediately if anything happened. I sat up a long time waiting for a messenger.

The camp was really surprised next morning when daylight showed the opposite hill perfectly bare which had been filled with tents and moving men the day before. Col T regretted not having permitted me to report and said he would tell Genl Lee about it. The Genl afterwards said I should have advanced the pickets and felt the enemy—just think if I had known that was the way to manage these things we should have had an exciting time that night.

The Confederates lost an incredible opportunity to attack when the evacuation of Rosecrans' fortifications went unreported. Like Floyd at Carnifex Ferry, Rosecrans was caught in a difficult position, with Lee and a numerically superior force in his front. The high water at Gauley Bridge had halted ferry operations and Rosecrans moved back toward his depots, shortening his supply lines as he moved closer to guns that could provide some protection for his force, if it came under attack, near the river crossing. If Lee attempted to move his entire force forward in pursuit, he would be stretching his supply lines to the point that his quartermasters would be unable to feed and supply the small Confederate army. Rosecrans had made the right tactical decision, but the risk had been great. If the alarm had been given as he evacuated his positions, the Federal force—at a minimum—would have lost its rear guard in a bloody battle. If Lee had been able to react with his limited cavalry force, the strung-out Union supply and artillery train would have also suffered severely.

As it was, the standoff on Sewell Mountain had come to an end.

chapter 4

COTTON HILL

"The enemy has got a battery opposite our post, and is shelling it! What d'ye think of that?"

—Rosecrans to Cox, November 1, 1861, regarding the conflict at Cotton Hill

Lee was now in an excellent position from which he could force the Union defenders from western Virginia, especially the Kanawha Valley and its crucial salt works, which were sorely needed by the Confederacy. The movement was planned on two fronts. First, Floyd would leave Sewell Mountain with his brigade and the regiments that had once belonged to his rival, Wise. Isaac Smith's worst fears were about to come true: he would again be serving under John B. Floyd. The second movement was to be under Lee's command, but this movement was canceled when Federal forces began to pressure the vital Shenandoah Valley from the west. Lee was forced to send W.W. Loring's troops back to the east, thereby reducing his effective strength.

There is some degree of mystery as to Lee's reason for allowing Floyd to continue with his unsupported march to the south side of New River to occupy positions from which he would be able to harass Rosecrans' army while lying protected behind the flood waters of the New and Kanawha Rivers. Moving with the commander who was widely despised by the men in the 22nd Virginia, Issac Smith began to record events once again after a delay. On October 27, 1861, from Cotton Hill, a position overlooking the Federal positions at Gauley Bridge, but on the opposite side of the flooded rivers, Smith wrote:

Don't recollect what stopped my writing before but will continue now.

COTTON HILL

Supposedly hunger had driven the enemy away. Our whole force remained here a number of days longer. Floyd was busy in getting up a scheme to enter the Kanawha Valley. At last we received orders to march on Friday I think (October 11th) by Richmond's Ferry. No information was given whether we were to cross New River or not or what our destination was. I ought to say that in the meantime I had again been detailed as Officer of the Day but this time went to headquarters and demanded a change which was readily made. We set out on Friday, marched slowly along through a rich and finely rolling hill country along the Sewell ridge. The land is positively excellent and nearly level. Traveled about eight miles [13km], stopped away down in the valley of a New River creek. It rained considerably and we had an unpleasant night. Next day marched about ten miles [16km] and stopped on Lick Creek (see it on the map). Camped here Saturday night—next day (Sunday) each regiment was ordered to send fifty men and two field officers to work on the road. Our regiment has but one and of course I had to go and was off at six o'clock, and actu-

PAGE 83: The Confederate standard bearer assumed the most dangerous position within his regiment. Centered at the front of his regiment, he drew a disproportionate amount of fire from the enemy. LEFT: In this untitled painting (1862) by William D. Washington, Confederate scouts watch the movements and preparations of the Union army. Food delivery, followed by increased periods of food preparation, generally indicated a troop movement was in the near future. ABOVE: Pickets on the road guarded the approach to the Federal post at Gauley Bridge. This representation was sketched by J. Nep Roessler.

ally worked hard until about 2:30 P.M. this evening. How often I thought of the dear ones at home, and the surprise they would feel if they knew how I was engaged, but it was my duty and unpleasant as it was I obeyed orders. The next day we marched to the ferry, our regiment in advance, the road barely wide enough for one wagon and where the road led down to New River, steep precipices were on the lower side— a misstep might have been fatal. The romance of the place is charming—to my surprise found New River here a broad stream as wide as our loved Kanawha flowing smoothly along its channel. Have an idea this is the place Uncle Bill and Aunt Ellen crossed at, though possibly it may have been at Pade's Ferry, higher up. We were occupied the larger part of the day crossing our troops and train but reached a point about 3 miles [5km] from the ferry on the South Side at which camp I commenced this sheet. We were here some time waiting the crossing of other troops. Thursday morning Oct 10th marched under orders for the turnpike some ten or twelve miles [16 or 19km] distant. Moved very slowly, the road being dreadfully cut up by the trains which preceded us and very indifferent originally. About three o'clock went down a big hill into a gloomy laurel hollow and found about 3 or 4 pieces of artillery with as many caissons and some 15 ordnance and baggage wagons closely packed in the same hollow and utterly unable to get up the terrible hill which led out of it. We had neither room nor authority to pass and in the midst of the rain which now set in awaited the movements of those before us. Col Tompkins had gone on ahead to select our camp ground on the turnpike 5

miles [8km] further on. After about two hours I ordered the men to pitch their tents upon the slippery hillside and we remained there all night. Awoke for an early start next morning but the wagons and guns were still there. Sent forward men to work the road around them and to help them up and finally about 3 o'clock in the evening set out ourselves. We had to help the other wagons before us and actually only marched about a mile and a half [2.5km] to the top of the hill. Col T met us on the way up and left us for Lewisburg to meet Mrs. Tompkins whom he had just learned was at that place. I was therefore in command of the regiment and dreaded the responsibility. Plus rode forward in great haste to tell Col Tompkins the news about his wife and the Col frequently alludes to it, says he will never forget Plus for his kindness.

While still a girl, Ellen Wilkins Tompkins had met a dashing artillery lieutenant on furlough from the Seminole wars and fell deeply in love, and soon they were married. They experienced periods of separation when the lieutenant—and soon after, captain—was assigned to faraway posts, absences that led to his resignation from the army in 1848. In 1855, the couple moved into the mountains where the trained engineer from West Point became involved in the coal industry, and the couple became leading citizens of the area. Once war became a reality, both husband and wife decided to support Virginia, his native state. Ellen had elected to remain on their large farm—an estate near Gauley Bridge—to ensure its safety as Union troops occupied the area.

Colonel Tompkins had written a letter to General Cox to request, as gentlemen did between them during that period, that the Federal officer assume responsibility for the

Ellen Tompkins, the wife of Christopher Tompkins, remained on her farm in western Virginia as the Confederate army withdrew to the east. At the request of Colonel Tompkins, Union General Cox assumed responsibility for the safety of Mrs. Tompkins and her children.

safety of his wife and children. Cox agreed and this same responsibility was honored by General Rosecrans as he assumed command in the area, but Ellen was restricted to her home and yard for her safety. An entire Union camp developed around her house and her lovely sixteen-year-old daughter, also named Ellen, was hidden from view of any of the Union soldiers. This was a dangerous time to be a young civilian woman without adult male protection. For example, Rutherford B. Hayes, who was Cox's adjutant general at that time, was also a military prosecutor; he used a room in the Tompkins house to try two German soldiers for rape.

While Ellen Tompkins was under the protection of both Cox and Rosecrans, most of the ordinary soldiers felt that she was treated too well. Even Hayes, a future president, argued that the home should be burned as a form of punishment for Tompkins' great crime, secession. Ellen and their children had been held on the farm from late July until October 14, when she was allowed "on a parole of honor" to travel to Richmond to get winter clothing for her children. It was at this time that Plus, actually named Noyes Rand, rode to alert Tompkins

of the release of his wife and that she was awaiting him in Lewisburg. She would return to their farm in mid-November, but would leave soon afterward when Floyd ordered artillery to be fired into the Union camp surrounding her home—with Ellen and the Tompkins children inside!

Now that Smith was the acting regimental commander of the 22nd Virginia, he was

entering dangerous waters: he would no longer have the experienced and politically connected Tompkins to shield him and the regiment under his command from the wrath of John B. Floyd.

Floyd knew that Tompkins despised him and furthermore that the officer had corresponded directly with General Lee about the former governor's misuse of the soldiers of the 22nd Virginia. Floyd, who was a vindictive man (to say the least), continued to place the 22nd in lead positions during attacks and in rear guard service when in retreat—the worst duties always came to the men of the 22nd Virginia. Floyd's dislike for them intensified after he had been slightly wounded at Carnifex Ferry and his rival, Henry A. Wise, called him a "Bullet Hit Son-of-a-Bitch" during a short speech in front of the 22nd Virginia. The soldiers' laughter at this publicly delivered jibe sealed their fate, if Floyd could ever arrange it. Smith wrote about the troubled march following the departure of his mentor Tompkins:

Taken early on in the war, this photograph of a soldier's camp shows better equipment than was usually available to most of the men in Confederate service. Union tents such as these surrounded the Tompkins' home at Gauley Mount.

Next morning, Saturday, marched from the turnpike expecting to go about four or five miles [6.5 or 8km], camp in a pleasant place with the troops ahead and await the arrival of those yet behind. Up to this time we knew nothing as to our destination. When about one mile [1.6km] from the turnpike Capt Jackson came up, said Genl Floyd had ordered all the troops forward and our regiment must join him as early as possible. Under this order I pushed the men and jaded teams along wretched roads to a point one mile east of Raleigh Court House in all about seventeen miles [27km] and the teams were very poorly fed before starting. Reported for orders and was told to keep my camp—found the other troops had orders to march at six o'clock next morning (Sunday) with

This illustration shows a division of Confederate cavalry at a halt. Floyd's small cavalry force suffered casualties as his army withdrew from the Cotton Hill region. St. George Croghan, the son of a War of 1812 hero, was killed while commanding Floyd's cavalry during the retreat from Cotton Hill.

two days rations cooked—was much surprised at our being left to rest. At about 9 next morning Floyd rode up, sent Plus to him for orders and he said we must move forward at once. In half an hour we were in motion, and that day we marched sixteen miles [26km], having nearly caught up with the troops who started 3 or 4 hours before us. All this haste was because Floyd had heard the enemy were at Fayette Court House. The men were thoroughly worn out, never saw them so used up. They could scarcely stand up long enough to receive orders for the night. Floyd camped about 150 yards from us across the creek and yet the order to cook provisions and march did not reach me until

11 o'clock that night. I determined not to awaken the poor fellows and did not, but had them up early the next morning. Could not possibly get off at the hour and could not get the cooked rations ordered the night before. Next morning learned the enemy were not on this side of the river and Floyd told me when I asked for a delay of an hour in my march that I must start at once and come on leisurely as the present state of things did not require the haste he had intended. The men declared it was impossible for them to march any distance and some thought they would not be able to move at all. We expected that all the troops would camp two miles [3km] east of Fayette Court House.

I went along leisurely with the men and about a mile [1.6km] this side of Fayette Court House found all the wagons of the troops stopped and learned that the troops had marched forward. This of course indicated an expected engagement. I inquired of everyone for any orders left for me, could get none, but I soon determined my course, left the wagons behind with the cooks and ordered provisions to be cooked and sent forward to the men. Told the men that the enemy were probably ahead and we must rush forward to be in the battle. Moved off and directly after met John Carr with orders from Col McCausland to bring up the men quickly and Carr said the Col had put his men to the double quick. Rode up and down the line to encourage the men. Cheered them up and got them off again at a quick trot and with a cheer. I was astonished that the poor, wearied men could move so readily and rapidly. We went on farther and farther and about two miles [3km] this side of the Court House I halted and made them

This fanciful illustration depicts several prominent Confederate leaders: Jefferson Davis (center), and (clockwise from top) General P.T.G. Beauregard, General Robert E. Lee, General Braxton Bragg, General Hollins, General Simon Bolivar Buckner, General A.S. Johnston, and General Joseph Johnston.

load. Finally about 4 or 5 miles [6.5 or 8km] from Fayette C.H. whilst I was encouraging the men forward expecting every moment to lead them into action, I was mortified and astonished to have Col McCausland ride up and without a word to me, commence giving commands to the regiment, actually assuming command. In a short time I mentioned the subject to him and said I presumed he took command as the senior officer of the Brigade. The 22nd and the 36th regiments have been brigaded and placed under the command of Col Tompkins and of course when Col Tompkins was absent Col McCausland would command the brigade. Col Mc said he did not act in that capacity, but Genl Floyd had sent him to aid me (of course I understood that). This depressed me greatly for I saw that it was an insult I should be obliged to notice. McCausland of course was bound to obey, but the order was so utterly contrary to all decency or propriety and Floyd cared for none of these things. The men and officers under my sole command had acted well, had given me no trouble, had obeyed my commands with readiness and deference in spite of the fact that I had pushed them most severely and had been obliged to speak more harshly to all of them than ever before. I had brought them forward with alacrity and enthusiasm and I am satisfied they

In this painting by Keith Rocco, a red sash shows beneath the uniform jacket of a Confederate artillery officer. These brave men were often called upon to position their guns where covering fire could be utilized to protect a retreat. Casualties were high among these men because they were often the target of the enemy's fire.

These Confederate caps show two of the styles commonly found within the southern army. Handmade clothing appeared throughout the ranks and as a result there was little uniformity to Confederate outfits, even within regiments.

Charles Pace, Company A, 18th Virginia Infantry, the "Danville Blues," poses in a prewar militia uniform. The gaiety of the costume highlights the difference between the prewar activities of such volunteer militia and the grim reality of their Civil War service.

would have followed me into battle with full confidence and reliance and just as we were nearing the point of danger another man is ordered to assume command over my troops and I am marched through two or three regiments ahead of us with a stranger, my superior, in command.

Floyd had managed to exact some of the revenge he had planned for the 22nd Virginia. His vindictiveness could not touch Tompkins, but in Tompkins' absence, the former governor set out to make the regiment look bad and embarrass the acting commander in front of both his peers and the men in his regiment. It was, as Smith put it, an insult he was obliged to notice. Unfortunately, it wasn't over:

We hurried on, and strange to tell, my poor wearied men without food or a moment's halt are pushed forward past men who are well rested and had food with them and were marched on, without stopping to within about 1¼ miles [2km] of the Kanawha River at a house on Fall's Creek, and about seven miles [11km] in advance of the other forces. We halted here, the enemy picket was at the turnpike on this side and their tents whitening every level spot on the other side of New River.

One hundred of this little band was sent on still farther as a picket with orders to push up as close to the enemy as possible. Our ranks of course were greatly thinned by many causes. We were out of the way of the relief seven miles behind. A cold rain had set in, the pickets were not allowed fires and they were to follow a road every turn of which might disclose an armed foe and if possible get sight of the river that

night. I was opposed to the position, but McCausland had command. The top of the mountain was a strong place and there I would have stopped if in command. When we did stop we were in a trap. The main body had marched 21 miles [34km] that day, the picket had advanced about a mile [1.6] further on the most dangerous duty in the service.

You can imagine the anxiety with which the night was passed, every moment we were expecting to hear the guns which would indicate our pickets had met. Early next morning, Col Mc and I went to visit the picket. Col Mc thought it had not advanced far enough and we undertook to push it farther. We moved down beyond our outside man, not knowing but that every turn of the road would bring a volley upon us and then planted the picket much nearer that it was before. This morning provisions came at last, the first the men had eaten in more than 24 hours. Every day seemed to convince me that our position was the most wretchedly chosen for our main body—and it was the subject of earnest consultation between some of the captains and myself and my views were pretty well known to Col Mc. The enemy seemed to know nothing of us and we actually pushed the picket almost to the last turn where the road turns down to the turnpike. On one morning I went to our outpost man, climbed a tree and thought I could plainly discern a sentinel about 150 yards [137m] off at the turnpike with his gun in his hand.

During our stay here in examining our position Col Mc, Capt Sam Miller, and myself and two others went along the ridge leading to Cotton Hill and looked down upon the enemy at Stockton's and Gauley and above all else could see the old Kanawha River and see it dashing along away down below. How my heart leaped to think how near the loved ones were and yet how far away. I looked on the noble stream and sent my heart.

A replacement bridge was erected over Gauley River to replace the covered structure ordered burned by Wise in July 1861. Prefabricated in Philadelphia and hauled to the construction site over mountain roads, the new suspension bridge carried Union army traffic until it was destroyed in September 1862. Cotton Hill can be seen in the background.

Major Smith and the men of the 22nd Virginia had been marched to exposed positions at the westernmost portion of what was soon to become a battlefield. Cotton Hill overlooked Rosecrans' positions and supply depots at Gauley Bridge, and the 22nd Virginia was now positioned near Montgomery's Ferry, just below the majestic falls in the Great Kanawha River. Union regiments were located near Stockton's Inn and their "tents whitening every level spot" on the northern shore of the river contained a large number of soldiers. Additional Federal regiments were positioned at Tompkins' farm on the western edge of Gauley Mountain as

Floyd's four thousand men began to prepare to shell them.

Smith's regiment was at the most exposed position in the Confederate line, placed there as an early warning for the rest of Floyd's regiments—including John McCausland's 36th Virginia—which were placed in the relative safety of the ridge line above the Kanawha River. Floyd's men were in their positions opposite Rosecrans' camps on the north side of the river and the Confederates began to drive the Union pickets who had crossed the river back from their assigned posts. Shortly afterwards, Floyd's cannon, which had been hauled disassembled on sledges by oxen, had been reassembled and the gunners were ordered to begin what would be a ten-day siege of the small town of Gauley Bridge. When something moved, Floyd's gunners fired at it. The ferry across the strategic river crossing was halted and Union troops moved at great risk during daylight. Nonetheless, General Cox and other Union officers crossed the flooded river on November 10 and were able to force the Confederate army, artillery and all, to withdraw, back in the direction of Raleigh Court House along the route over which they had come into the region.

Floyd again had very narrowly escaped total destruction as a three-pronged attack came very close to encircling his small army. He began a winter retreat over muddy roads, a withdrawal that was perhaps one of the worst (in terms of the hardships suffered by the soldiers) of the entire war.

Isaac Smith had been busy trying to survive the wrath of John B. Floyd while at the same time seeing to the needs of his men. Not surprisingly, the harassment of the young major with the prominent Unionist father gained in intensity in the absence of Colonel Tompkins. Becoming truly miserable, the young officer began writing again in his diary on November 9:

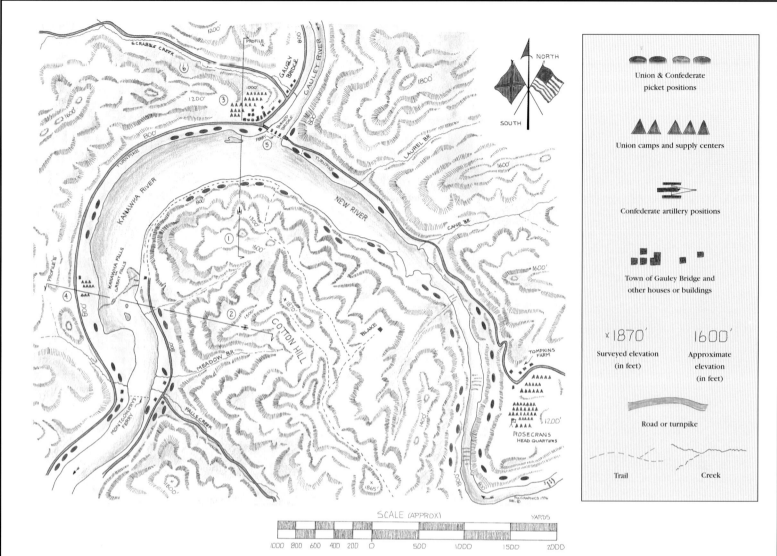

Legend:

Union & Confederate picket positions

Union camps and supply centers

Confederate artillery positions

Town of Gauley Bridge and other houses or buildings

×1870' Surveyed elevation (in feet)

1600' Approximate elevation (in feet)

Road or turnpike

Trail   Creek

SCALE (APPROX)   YARDS

1000 800 600 400 200 0   500   1000   1500   2000

THE SIEGE OF GAULEY BRIDGE (NOVEMBER 1–7, 1861)—OVERHEAD VIEW OF UNION AND CONFEDERATE EMPLACEMENTS

1 and 2. Confederate artillery on Cotton Hill. On October 27, Confederate forces under General John B. Floyd establish commanding artillery positions opposite the Union supply base near the town of Gauley Bridge and overlooking the Union camp at Kanawha Falls.

3. Union camp and stores at Gauley Bridge. From November 1–6, Union forces at Gauley Bridge are shelled by Confederate artillery placed near the top of Cotton Hill. The siege is finally lifted on November 7, when long-range parrot guns open fire on Confederate positions, compelling the Rebels to withdraw.

4. Union camp at Kanawha Falls. Throughout the siege, this camp is under fire. Beginning on November 4, all other Union camps near Hawks Nest are regularly shelled as well.

5. Gauley Bridge ferry. Union troops at Gauley Bridge operate a ferry until a new bridge is built in January 1862. In September of the same year, the bridge is destroyed again, this time by retreating Union troops.

6. Scrabble Creek Valley. Confederate artillery fire forces Union troops to move their stores and ammunition into the valley for protection.

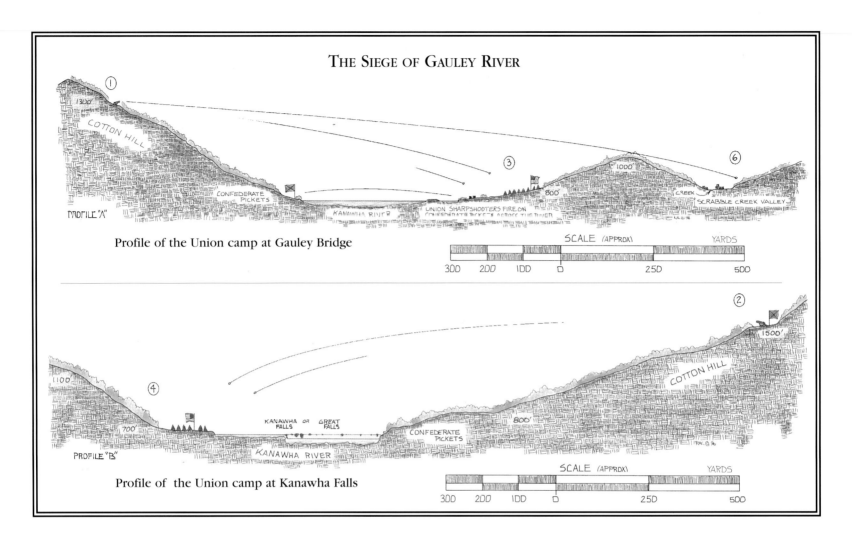

Profile of the Union camp at Gauley Bridge

SCALE (APPROX)
YARDS
300 200 100 0 250 500

Profile of the Union camp at Kanawha Falls

SCALE (APPROX)
YARDS
300 200 100 0 250 500

Many misfortunes have befallen me since I last wrote here. Something stopped me suddenly, I know not what at this time.

I have felt unwilling to continue this little history, as it involves so much of my unhappiness and trials, and nothing but utter want of employment now permits me to write. Without employment my thoughts are painful. But I will hurry over these events.

On Thursday (I think) just after dinner, we were all sitting quietly in Huddleston's house, the men lounging about outside and in without their guns.

So long a time had elapsed during our stay at this dangerous place, without anything of moment occurring, that we all felt much more secure; true the picket had fired twice on Yankees who had sauntered up the road, but the Yanks seemed to pay no attention to our presence here. That morning two men had been fired on, in a most shameful manner, and suffered to escape after they had surrendered themselves, but it had taken place early in the morning and no notice was taken of it.

Suddenly the rattling crash of musketry was heard all around us, and the

greatest uproar and confusion prevailed. Men were crowding in the house, others rushing out all confused and (I may well say as to many of them) terrified. I was upstairs, and seizing my sword and pistol, rushed out to make my way down; the narrow staircase was a perfect jam, men rushing up with and after their guns, and often seeking to get out. I found it impossible to get out. An effort to do so would have impaled me upon the bayonets, which were bristling above the heads of the men. I stood at the head of the stairs urging the men to get their guns and clear the house. Finally forced

"Pain bullets" were recovered from locations where the wounded of both sides received medical treatment. Lacking pain relievers of any sort (except for alcohol), the wounded were given lead bullets upon which to bite in an effort to control their pain. Given the depth of some of the bite marks in these bullets, the injured soldiers must have been in agony. The expression "biting the bullet" arose from this practice.

my way through the mass and rushed out into the road. To my surprise and mortification, the men were flying in every direction. I had no idea where the enemy was, supposed they occupied the hills on both sides of the hollow, and had surrounded us. Couldn't see the enemy though. They were firing continually, and some of our men were firing back. A few men had taken their station (Mr. Quarrier prominent among them) under the bank in front of the house. Found out pretty soon that the enemy were only at the hill in front of the house, and immediately ordered those brave fellows to fall back that we might occupy the hill on the opposite side. They fell back and we found a stone fence

Counterattack—The West Woods, *by Keith Rocco, depicts the breakthrough of Confederate troops once a Federal assault stalled and was turned back to its starting point. As this painting illustrates, the soldiers of the poorly supplied southern army attempted to compensate for their material disadvantages with displays of exceptional valor.*

would fill our purpose better and halted there. Just then for the first time, I saw the enemy though I had been exposed to their fire for some time, and immediately jumped on the stone wall and called upon the men to follow me, and charge up the hill upon them. I stood urging the men for some seconds before any of them came. Young Reynolds says whilst standing there he saw a minie ball strike right at my feet which dashed dirt into his eyes as he came up to me. The boys came up following me, and the enemy who had begun to run were soon out of sight. I sent two large parties out to intercept them, but they escaped. Their trace where they crossed the hill on their return was bloody, showing they had wounded men along. They left one fellow dead in the field shot in the center of the forehead, and one mortally wounded through the body. We had one man shot slightly through the foot and another scratched in the hand. The house had a number of bullets through it. I felt great pity for the wounded man, he was in great agony—about 20 and fine-looking, fair skin, dark hair, and intelligent face. I talked to him kindly— he said he would soon die.

The enemy had crossed the hill behind our pickets, and thus surprised us. I had expected them to surprise us in some such way for it was impossible for us to guard against it.

McCausland who had not been with us since the night before soon came up, and to my gratification gave it as his opinion that we ought to leave immediately and go to the top of the hill. I told him my opinion had always been that the top was the only proper place for us, and we drew in our pickets, and moved off at once. I went up the hollow and made provision for having the wounded

man taken care of, and the dead man buried—fixed both in the best way we could. The poor fellow died about midnight as I since know.

On the hill we were without tents, and but little fire and bitter cold.

Isaac Smith had survived another skirmish with the Union army as the acting commander of the 22nd Virginia. He had allowed his men to relax while they were placed in a very exposed position with reinforcements too far away to aid them quickly. Part of this was due to his relative inexperience, and part was due to the distraction of having Floyd persecute him and his regiment, in particular by giving command of the regiment to McCausland. Smith's guard was down when the Union army patrol opened fire on his unprepared soldiers, but they were lucky—they might have fared far worse had the Federal com-

mander sent a larger force to attack the careless 22nd Virginia.

Smith may have felt vindicated by the move that McCausland ordered that took the men to cheerless positions on the ridge overlooking their former location, but bad news was on its way to Isaac Smith. He continued to record events in his diary:

On Friday Col Tompkins came at last, and brought me Pa's letter with Maj Parks' papers, and Ma's excellent letter. I read with much concern. Col Tompkins heard how I was treated, and was very much vexed—he knew that I intended to resign in consequence, and I told him so again, he thought no other course possible or admissible. I had only waited for his return in order to resign. That night we heard of Clarkson's return from a trip down the Kanawha, and Plus whispered to me that

During the Civil War, and particularly in its initial stages, both sides were using similar equipment, which many soldiers had received during service in the prewar national army. These items—an 1840-issue cavalry saber (nicknamed "wristbreaker") with scabbard and a short-barreled revolver holster—are good examples of such ubiquitous equipment, though in this case they belonged to Confederate soldiers.

the captured Poll books had Pa's name as a candidate. I need not say how this intelligence grieved me—his friends all said they were satisfied that he had not authorized it and said so I fondly hoped. I saw too that this fact was to have an unfortunate influence upon my resignation. That night I was very sad. Next day my resignation was handed in. Sunday passed and I heard nothing, but that Gen. Floyd had forwarded it to the Department for acceptance without comment, which insures prompt acceptance. Next day, Monday,

I applied for the usual leave of absence granted on such occasions and on Tuesday received an order giving me leave. This I supposed happily ended the matter. I was forced however to remain several days to settle up my affairs. I had just paid 200 dollars for a horse, now useless to me, had just received a saddle and bridle for which I paid 60 dollars about two months before, had a uniform on the way for which I had paid 85 dollars at the same time and another military saddle for which I paid 35 dollars. I remained here to sell these

articles. On Thursday, Ben Turner and John Noyes arrived, and heard the startling intelligence that Pa was actually and fully identified with the Pierpont government. Those with whom I was connected call and curse him as a traitor, and he surely knew it would surely be so. Why my dear father had chosen to place me in this terrible situation is beyond my comprehension. I have been shocked beyond description in contemplating the awful consequences to the peace, safety, and happiness of both of us. I cannot write all that crowds upon my mind .... It is all terrible.

The other soldiers mentioned were also members of the Kanawha Riflemen and they had apparently slipped back to their homes inside Union territory for a short visit. Clarkson had managed to capture some poll books that listed Benjamin Smith as a candidate for a position within the Pierpont administration, a group of Unionists who had claimed to be the rightful government of the entire state of Virginia. These loyalists were hated by the people and soldiers who had chosen to remain loyal to the current government of Virginia and the secessionist movement. This was difficult news for Isaac Smith to bear and he must have had a sleepless night after hearing this, but far worse tidings were on their way. He continued to write:

On that morning Wm Quarrier who had also just reached here told me that General Davis at Headquarters would buy my horse. I immediately rode there. Whilst there the Adjutant handed me an order revoking my furlough, and ordering me to rejoin my regiment. I was astonished. Went to Floyd for an explanation. At first he endeavored to put me off with an unjust insinuation about my resigning in the presence of the enemy

Mostly printed in the North, newspapers (shown being distributed among the troops) that were delivered in camp were often the sole source of information on the progress of the war as a whole for the ordinary soldiers. Freedom of the press, however, was seen as a nuisance by many commanders as these newspapers were excellent sources of intelligence for the Confederates.

Confederate money was minted and issued by states and local authorities without thought of the inflation its use would cause. It quickly became practically worthless, and many consumers chose to use Federal "greenbacks" and gold instead.

come. Col Tompkins insisted I should have a Court of Inquiry, but that involves a six or twelve months task in attending to it. I have been expecting ever since to be ordered on dangerous service, for the malignity of the man who could take pleasure in keeping father and son in open hostility is ready for anything.

and when an engagement was expected, knowing as he well did that it was the gross insult he had put upon me, and my regiment, that forced me to resign, and that I awaited Col Tompkins' return, under great exposure to danger, and experiencing the only fighting we have had here where there was a danger, before I offered to resign.

I insisted on more explicitness, then began a conversation in which was evinced the coarsest brutality, the most outrageous tyranny, injustice and meanness. He grew excited and angry, used his position and rank to treat me with the coarsest severity, knowing that I could not resist. He declared that my father was engaged in an effort to defeat the great cause in which his army (and I was a member of it) was struggling

and had made himself a traitor, and that he intended I should remain in the Confederate army as long as he could possibly keep me there, that I should stand in the front of battle, and meet my father face to face—that he would immediately write to the Department not to accept my resignation, and keep me here. This and much more was said in a most brutal and unfeeling manner, and here I am held as a sort of hostage or prisoner, yet pretending to command a regiment. I could write pages on this affair, for I have suffered most intensely under it—but I have learned that an opportunity of sending my letters can be had today, and I must hasten. Here I have remained since that day, perfectly miserable. I am hoping for deliverance in a day or two, but fear it will not

Floyd was the type of commander dreaded by soldiers. Quick to anger and unreasonable while angry, Floyd didn't forgive and once he had made up his mind about someone, it was usually too late to save the victim. He used the security provided by rank and position to harass his victims, but had they been of equal rank it is likely that a man such as Christopher Tompkins would have challenged his actions. Isaac Smith, a western Virginia volunteer, had several shortcomings in the eyes of Floyd. First, he was a friend and subordinate of Tompkins, a West Point graduate who held Floyd in open contempt. Second, Smith may have been viewed by Floyd as being responsible for the escape of Rosecrans at Sewell Mountain. And third, Smith's father was a prominent Unionist who supported Francis Pierpont, a loyal Unionist who had laid claim to the governor's seat in Richmond, a position recently held by Floyd himself. When Smith attempted to resign, Floyd felt he had sufficient authority to attempt to destroy the young officer.

Smith sensed his peril and began anticipating orders that would lead him and his regiment into "dangerous service," that is, a fatal mission that would be the ultimate conclusion to the conflict between him and Floyd.

Isaac Smith's position was to worsen even further as his friend and commander resigned from service. Tompkins had requested a leave from his duties in order to get his family relocated to Richmond, a reasonable request that Floyd refused. Consequently,

Confederate officers, like this one on horseback, endured much hard service during the Civil War. Exposure to the elements and their tendency to personally lead their men into battle produced great numbers of casualties among their officer corps. Thus, perhaps the most hazardous of all occupations was that of the Confederate general officer.

Tompkins resigned his commission and left the area—without any of the complications suffered by Smith. As noted before, Tompkins had strong friends and allies in Richmond and so could depend upon a speedy and relatively trouble-free passage through any Confederate-controlled territories.

Smith continued to explain in his diary about events surrounding the ending of the fighting at Cotton Hill:

Our regiment remained on the mountain until ordered out after a party of Yankees, who appeared within our lines and we marched 11 or 12 miles [18 or 19km] in rain and cold over the roughest hills, brush, rocks and cliffs—were lost—staid all night on top of a high hill, could get no farther, were hungry and cold without shelter—and reached our comfortless camp about 11 o'clock next day, more than 24 hours without food. We are now camped in the hollow, but the men have their arduous duty to perform in the hills.

On Wednesday last Col Tompkins asked for leave of absence to make arrangements for his family in Richmond—his means had been lost to him by the war, and he needed to make some provisions to provide their necessities. This leave was refused him, and he resigned and has gone, leaving my condition much more hopeless and miserable than before. I, a prisoner commanding men who were commanded by so excellent a Colonel, and the men placed in circumstances making the command infinitely more difficult.

I shall close for the present. I demand that nothing written here shall be read outside the family and that any statements here about the army shall be kept strictly secret, though I have endeavored throughout to avoid mentioning any

facts which would be prejudicial to the interests of the Confederate States. I am aiming to give a sort of personal narrative of what has befallen me in this campaign more than a history of the war.

An attorney in civilian life, Smith knew the importance of minimizing any advantage that Floyd could gain through the confiscation and perusal of the diary. Now that Smith's father had been denounced as a traitor, the new commander of the 22nd Virginia Infantry Regiment began to fear that Floyd might accuse him of espionage. Entries in the diary could have been used as evidence against him, and with emotions running high against Benjamin Smith, Isaac Smith might have had some difficulty in proving that he was loyal to the Confederacy. The resignation of his commander, Colonel Tompkins, removed the thin shield that had served to protect Smith from the total wrath of Floyd. The above final paragraph was probably intended as a disclaimer, should the diary be confiscated and examined. Isaac Smith was beginning to take as few chances as possible when dealing with his powerful enemy as he tried to lead his regiment, composed of men who were both friends and relatives. Smith continued to document the activities on Cotton Hill:

I remained in command of the regiment, nothing of moment occurring until Sunday, Nov 10th, when Col Wm A. Jackson of Charleston, of the Jenny Lind back street, was assigned to the command of the regiment. This relieved me very much as all the responsibility and annoyance was shifted to his shoulders. Poor man, he had nothing in the world—not a blanket, no towel, soap, or any indispensibles of camp life. I shared my scanty stock with him. That night at about one o'clock he received orders to

have everything ready for a movement at daylight next morning. Were ready accordingly and after some time were ordered to march to the rear—went about one mile [1.6km] back and were drawn up in order of battle to await an attack of the enemy (if any was made) whilst the guns on Cotton Hill which had been playing Hot Ball across the river for about a week could be extricated. These guns had been placed in position with great difficulty and had to be watched continually by 300 to 500 men exposed to every hardship and had been firing away thousands of dollars worth of ammunition and so far as I knew or heard never struck anything or did anyone any harm. The guns were finally extricated (and the enemy deserves to be sneered at for permitting it) and we moved on about 3 or 4 miles [5 or 6.5km] and encamped at what was said to be a very strong position. We had just fairly gotten our tents pitched when the enemy began to fire shells into our camp from the opposite cliff of New River. It rather struck some of the army that under such circumstances the position was not so terribly strong after all. However we put up breastworks working after night and next day some men were sent down to feel the enemy and we were kept at the breastworks. At about eleven o'clock A.M. the enemy began to shell us again and they shot very handsomely, too. Their range was exact upon the camp of the 22nd and the 36th—we could not get our wagons and horses in any position to keep out of harm's way. One shell fell under a wagon but did not burst—a large piece of an exploded shell fell about 20 steps from our tent where we were at dinner and about 5 or 6 steps from our wagon and horses. The firing was not kept up by the enemy or they could have damaged us greatly.

The enemy were no longer to be sneered at as they were beginning a counterattack that would shortly imperil Floyd's entire army. Rosecrans had divided his force, sending one brigade under General Schneck upstream to cross New River and move against Floyd's rear from the east. At the same time, he ordered General Benham to move a full brigade downstream approximately eight miles (13km) and cross the Kanawha River—an extension of the Kanawha after New River joined with Gauley River at Gauley Bridge—and move into Floyd's rear from the west. He ordered the simultaneous movement of part of Cox's force to cross the Kanawha at the base of Cotton Hill to hold the attention of Floyd's force as the other brigades got into their rear. This excellent plan would have resulted in the capture of most of Floyd's little army, but Schneck's brigade was unable to cross because of high water and was ordered to the west to reinforce Benham. Benham, however, was slow to move into position. The tardy response by Benham gave Floyd's men an opportunity to escape and Isaac Smith wrote about the retreat:

About dusk a council of war was called and about 8 o'clock we were ordered to pack up wagons and prepared for marching. News had reached camp that the enemy had gotten in behind us and we were to retreat at once. A number of regiments had no transportation and were obliged to burn nearly everything they had. We were in the rear with the 36th and saw piles of tents, with broken cooking utensils and articles of every description blazing away as all had to be consumed and destroyed. As we marched along that night we could see

Confederate outposts (as in this portrait by Keith Rocco) housed the picket reserves, who were frequently rotated. Inspecting these positions was an especially hazardous duty for the officer of the day, and Smith reported that several men had been accidentally shot by their own pickets while performing this duty at Sewell Mountain. Their nerves stretched to the breaking point by long periods of isolation, pickets began to shoot suddenly at any movement.

where the flour had been thrown away, tents and along the line of march blankets, overcoats, and etc even were destroyed and many of our poor ragged fellows got hold of some good things thus thrown away. We trudged through the mud and cold, and stopped next day at about 11 o'clock A.M. after a march of about 15 miles [24km]. It is impossible to tell what became of all the sick and stragglers. I fear many of them have fallen into the hands of the enemy.

On Thursday, Nov 14th, continued our march, a heavy rain began to fall shortly after our start and the road (before most wretched) became a mass of liquid mud (such as the streets of Charleston in mid-winter) through which the poor soldiers were obliged to wade. We had not marched far before a courier pushed through the ranks at full speed hunting General Floyd and shortly after he appeared returning to the camping ground and gave us orders to halt at a place designated further on and about 5 miles [8km] from where we had camped the night before. We than heard of the skirmish in which Col Crogan was killed and that the enemy were about to attack our rear. This was a very dismal camp ground. I felt very anxious about our baggage. Every regiment had lost a large part of their equipments. We had lost none but rather gained, for our fellows picked up everything valuable and carried it. I was very anxious to have the wagons move on so that the old 22nd could come out of the campaign right side up.

Col Jackson had it arranged finally that the wagons should move on that night. After some time we found that all the trains were to move forward, and all the troops but the 22nd and 36th. We were to remain and in the morning

Confederate buglers provided loud, clear communication among widely spread military elements (while the Union also used buglers, they had the advantage of telegraph technology). Verbal commands and visual signals were normally impractical due to the distances involved, so the bugler's role in combat was vital.

fight the enemy from a position some distance back and after checking them fall back to another point where we would find another regiment and some artillery and there we were to make a decided stand.

Floyd had decided, again, to use the volunteers from western Virginia, the 22nd and 36th Virginia regiments, for the dangerous rear guard duty. They were once again judged to be expendable and they were to march toward near certain destruction in combat with Benham's advance force. The ordinary soldiers in the ranks were probably feeling much like Smith at this point as they had been misused by the finely dressed and equipped officers from east of the mountains

throughout the entire campaign. The morale of this rear guard force must not have been exceptionally high as the orders were given to them.

They had all heard of the death of Colonel St. George Crogan, Floyd's cavalry commander. An excitable officer, he had been nicknamed "Panic" by some of the volunteers under his command, but he was the son of one of the few genuine heroes of the War of 1812 and he did his duty to the last. General Benham, the commander of the men who killed Crogan, had known the father while a student at West Point and he arranged for the return of the body to the family for burial. As this incident illustrates, this conflict was, to paraphrase Isaac Smith, a most unusual war.

Smith continued to write about the pending rear guard action and his worst night of the war:

The night was cold and dark, the black clouds filled the heavens. Our tents were taken down and the wagons sent off to make their way through the mass of mud in front, if possible, and if not to be destroyed. The Quartermaster General was utterly and hopelessly drunk. Miller had great difficulty to keep away from him so as to manage his train in his own way. Very soon the heavy rain began to fall. I laid down on some straw, covered up head and feet with my old shaggy blanket and the rain poured down upon us in torrents. The most vivid lightning and tremendous peals of thunder were seen and heard every few moments. Added to all this the Officer who was to command us the next morning was foolishly drunk, perfectly childish and silly. I regard my position that night as the most unfortunate of my life. It seemed that God was against me, and I felt the contest of the morning would be fatal to me. The great probability of the destruction of our train, the personal discomforts of my position, the gross injustice and tyranny which placed me there, God's terrible presence in the heavens, the anticipated desperate fight of the morning and a drunken commander seemed to leave no hope, no prospect of escape. I was not afraid as cowards are, for this war, I believe, has assured me that I am not afraid of the battlefield, but I was superstitious and felt God had turned against me. With all this (thanks to my good old blanket) I slept soundly and sweetly during a part of the night. I surrendered my fate to my heavenly father and slept in peace. Plus slept by my side and poor fellow seemed to feel much as I did. Our situation was truly desolate.

Smith and the other volunteers were in a desperate situation as they waited to be attacked by superior forces that would have the support of both artillery and cavalry. Artillery could be expected when Union gunners began to shell them, weakening the Confederates for an infantry assault, and the Federal cavalry arm would be more than able to destroy or capture any of the soldiers who attempted to withdraw or retreat. Larger forces were converging on them from two directions and Cox's soldiers had already fought Floyd's men on the top of Cotton Hill at Blake's Farm.

The terrible storm had a demoralizing effect on the tired, hungry men in the ranks and the actions of the unnamed commander who was drunk and "perfectly childish and silly" did little to inspire the Confederate soldiers to perform great deeds. Nonetheless, Smith and his loyal friend and excellent soldier, Noyes Rand (a.k.a. Plus), remained with the men of the 22nd Virginia and prepared to do their duty against fearful odds:

Forward the Colors, *by Don Troiani, depicts the heroism and perseverance of the Confederate officer, who normally led from the front of his formation, placing himself in the most exposed position in an effort to inspire his men. Bravery was well respected by these soldiers, and they could normally be called upon to accomplish nearly impossible tasks, in part thanks to the example of their military leaders.*

Next morning all were astir. Plus and I were the only persons with dry clothes in the officer's mess. We marched off through the mud just at dawn to meet the enemy. Took our positions to await the attack. We could see far down the road from our elevated position and watched for the enemy with some eagerness (for strange to say there is a sort of excitement in battle, which makes a man rather court the contest, when the first anxiety has passed away) but we watched in vain. At 9 o'clock no enemy in sight and cavalry scouts reported none within 1½ [2.5km] miles. We were marched back to the second position, reported how matters stood and were ordered on.

Incredibly, the commander of the Federal forces in pursuit was slow in developing a plan to follow and engage the retreating Confederates. Cox had crossed Cotton Hill and was moving toward Floyd's men, but General Benham, a former engineer captain in the regular army, moved too slowly. Rosecrans sent impatient orders to him, but these did little good. General Cox later wrote: "Rosecrans had informed Benham of my advance and ordered him to push forward; but he spent the day discussing topography which he was supposed to have learned before....It would appear that Floyd did not learn of Benham's presence...until the 12th, when he began his retreat, and that at any time during the preceding week a single rapid march would have placed Benham's brigade without resistance upon the line of the enemy's communications. Rosecrans was indignant at the balking of his elaborate plans, and ordered Benham before a court-martial for misconduct." McClellan was responsible for having the charges dropped, and so Benham escaped the court-martial, but it was too late to

catch Floyd. The lucky former governor had escaped again.

Smith went on with his description of the rest of the retreat:

On this march we saw the true character of our retreat. The road and road side was strewn with articles of every description—tents, boxes, guns, clothes, provisions, knapsacks, broken harness, cooking utensils, dishes. Wagons were left fast in the mud with their loads untouched—at one place twelve wagons were left, most of them turned upside down, and at the same time a number of horses had drowned in the mud, that

This photograph shows Kanawha Falls near Gauley Bridge, where the Union army maintained a hospital and a wagon shop. A magazine was stocked at nearby Zoll's Hollow (near the center of the photograph); it was detonated in September 1862 to keep the ammunition from falling into Confederate hands.

is had sunk beyond hope of extrication and had been shot. At some places mudholes were filled with tents to make a passage for the wagons. All this was a perfect harvest of the 22nd. Being in front of the regiment, we noticed that this was only a fragment following up, and halted for the stragglers to catch up, waited a long time and they did not appear—went back and found the fellows resting behind. The rascals claimed to be tired down as a reason for their halt, and no wonder, for when I started them out again I found about every other man loaded down with flour, frying pans, buckets, mess kettles, and such things. I found myself eleven good percussion guns, and gave them to the men, but made them carry their flintlocks also. This regiment has by captures from the enemy and otherwise, gained about 100 good percussion guns, a number of them Enfield rifles. Had I commenced earlier, I would have secured many more guns, but it never occurred to me the men would leave their guns. Those that were left so far as I know were those of sick men turned over to the Master of Ordnance or which could not be transported with the men.

We camped that night (Friday) about two miles [3km] this side of Raleigh Court House—heavy snow that night. Many of the poor fellows are entirely barefoot, or nearly so as to make what they wear an encumbrance rather than a benefit. I begged from a Georgia Col four pairs of shoes for some poor fellows who had been marching barefoot, with their feet bleeding almost as they walked. These political brigadiers give every comfort and privilege first to their own troops, who take good care to leave nothing for the poor Va Vols who have been a sort of shuttlecock between them.

"Battle peeling" was a practice reported in the northern newspapers, the accounts of which were often accompanied by provocative images to titillate and outrage the readers. Stripping the dead was a fairly common practice late in the war, when underequipped Confederate troops had to scrounge in order to clothe and arm themselves, but it was not as common as readers of contemporary newspapers might have thought. By frequently running reports of battle peeling, the papers sought to demonize the Confederates for their original sin, the "great crime of secession."

Smith had requested a furlough at Cotton Hill and had been denied; to his credit, he remained faithfully with the soldiers of his regiment, many of them men from his home territory. He fondly referred to them as "rascals," as if they were tardy schoolboys rather than soldiers collecting supplies that had been abandoned by better equipped regiments. He "begged" for shoes for several of his men who were marching along with bleeding, bare feet and yet refused to drop out or surrender. There was good reason to be proud of these men, who had poor equipment and were chronically short of food and supplies: they had led the army in

attack, followed the army in retreat, and built breastworks for the entire regiment with a meager four axes.

Isaac Smith personally recovered eleven rifles that had been abandoned, and regretted not trying to get more. This level of concern for his men is remarkable from an officer who was trying to resign and was being harassed by his commanding general. He didn't seem to think twice, but continued to take his responsibilities seriously. Obviously, duty was more than just a word to Major Isaac Smith.

Smith returned to writing in his diary on November 16:

"We moved on about two miles [3km] where all of the troops were camped. Sunday (a happy day for me) late in the afternoon Col Jackson came from Headquarters, and handed me a paper. I opened it supposing it was some order relative to the troops generally and read (and with what delight) the order from the Secy of War accepting my resignation. I immediately began to fix up, and Monday morning at about 9 o'clock bid farewell to the 22nd and as I hoped military life forever. I was determined to let no delay give an opportunity to Floyd for further persecution. Came to Pack's Ferry in Monroe County that night (that I am sure is the place where Uncle Bill and Aunt Ellen traveled)—from thence I came last night to this place where I happened to see old Mr. Henderson of Pt. Pleasant. He told me I could get lodging at this house, and I am now comfortably fixed by a great fire writing to the loved ones at home. This morning the rain was falling fast and I had some of the most utterly filthy (no other words will suit) clothes to have washed, I determined to remain here a day more especially as I have no particular purpose or destination in view. At Mr. Pack's house I ate under a roof and slept in a bed for the first time since the middle of August, when we left White Sulphur. The luxury of these two things is perfectly tremendous and overpowering. And now how can I be sufficiently grateful to the Merciful God, who has brought me thus far in perfect safety and health through so many hardships and trials. May God give me grace to praise him for his mercies, and trust him for deliverance from all troubles.

Clearly, Isaac Smith was pleased with his release from service under John B. Floyd, particularly since he had managed to get away relatively unscathed. But it wasn't luck alone that had secured the acceptance of his resignation. As the regiment's commander, he had been able to arrange for one of his men to travel to Richmond to lobby on his behalf, apparently using family or personal connections in the Confederacy's capital. Smith explained how he had earlier taken matters into his own hands:

The day that Floyd revoked my furlough I made arrangements to send Wm. Quarrier to Richmond to secure the acceptance of my resignation. He and Miller and myself fully agreed that was the better course. The next morning, Nov 1st, he left.

Now freed from service, Smith was soon in a major town, Lewisburg, and he was able to go to church for the first time since he left his home. He continued to write in his diary from Lewisburg on November 24, 1861:

Came to this place on Friday, and am at the hotel with a good room, but the country is so eaten out by soldiers that one nearly starves at the hotel. This is the Sabbath day, and I thank God from my heart that I have been permitted once more to visit his holy sanctuary, and hear Jesus Christ and him crucified preached. The religious destruction of the army is awful, and I have felt my heart swell with thankfulness of this day (wickedly as I have spent it) for the grace which permits me to be where God's holy name and day are honored. Am waiting here for the evening church bell to ring, but it is now almost too late—the snow storm has doubtless prevented service tonight. Will probably go up to Mr. Matthews, and sit with Misses Jennie M. and C., our acquaintances of

Richmond. Called on them yesterday and they made many kind inquiries of Callie and Emma. This day finished the bible, fourth time of regular reading. Began either on my wedding day or the day after.

This is my wedding anniversary. How strange that the day which gave me my dear wife should upon its recurrence find us separated so far and with so little hope of meeting. How little any of that gay throng which assembled to witness the completion of our happiness anticipated the misery which has followed so soon. Oh, how this day especially makes us long for home, for my long-lost wife and the other dear ones. Poor Callie, you cannot feel the pangs of to-day's separation more than I and you

cannot realize the bitterness so deeply for you do not know the difficulties yet to be surmounted ere we can meet again.

I am boarding at this place—after some disappointment in my efforts to get cheap boarding in the country. I have settled here and am very comfortable. Mr. Arbuckle has no children but has an adopted nephew whom they raised from an infant eight days old. Both he and his wife are kind and pleasant and well-informed. They have a number of excellent books which I cannot more than finish in a year's stay. They keep an excellent table—plenty of milk, honey, butter and all the excellences of a good farm and have them cooked particularly well. The house is one of those time-

Some survivors of the 22nd Virginia are shown here in late 1865. Back row, left to right: Thomas Broun, Thomas Smith, Sam Miller, Thomas Fife, and Nicholas Fitzhugh. Front, left to right: Joseph Watkins, William Quarrier, Richard Laidley, and John Swann.

On November 30, Smith wrote an entry that described the difficulties that now faced him, a former field officer of the Confederacy, of conscription age, whose family lived in Union-controlled territory:

Went to town today and heard about Mr. N B Cabell's family starting for Kanawha. I shall again make an effort to send home this diary. I am applying for leave to come home, not that it is necessary to obtain leave, but that no one can say I have slyly deserted a cause, in which I have borne arms, or sneaked away from it. My hope is to find some quiet spot, where with Callie, parents, and sisters, we may all live through this terrible war, without participating in it. My intentions and desires will all be disclosed to this government.

My great trouble will probably be with the Yankees. Will they permit me to live under the jurisdiction of the U.S. simply upon parole not to bear arms against them, during the war, and can there be any certainty that the government will not repudiate the acts of their generals when it suits their convenience? I believe Genl Rosecrans would appreciate my position, but he is not President. I cannot take any oaths, but I do not expect to take up arms again. Apart from my own wishes on the subject, I could not do so with any propriety, maddened as the people are against my father.

It is impossible for me to say whether my unfortunate situation here will be so far appreciated to secure me the permission I seek. I hope it may, but even then a long time must elapse, and many difficulties overcome before I can find out what the Yankees would do with me.

As the saying goes, Smith was out of the frying pan and into the fire.

Soldier's Return, by A.D.O. Braivere, depicts the joy of the long-awaited homecoming of a husband and father from Civil War service. Sons and fathers from western Virginia were away from home and family for very long periods—many for the entire war.

honored log house structures with good sized fireplaces and large hearths where a big blazing fire is always ready to greet you. The floor undulating to a remarkable degree tells of old age and seems to be the more comfortable for its very irregularity. I am located in a newer part of the house—in fact I have the parlor which is snugly and neatly furnished. My bedroom opens into it and there I have everything as neat and comfortable as one could wish (linen sheets), a luxury unheard of by me since my departure from home until now. Mr. Arbuckle has a splendid farm, 2000 acres [800ha] of the best land in Greenbrier. Many of the fields are now covered with the most magnificent grass, long enough to mow if not so trampled or fallen down. You can see I am comfortable and my poor horse is literally "in clover." All of these comforts only serve to remind me the more of Callie and home.

chapter 5

The Making of a Confederate Spy

Isaac Smith was now out of the army, but he was unable to go home. He was fully aware of what had happened to Major Parks when the latter had come under the authority of Federal officials (he was imprisoned at Wheeling)—and Parks had had a safe conduct pass issued by General Cox. Smith feared this would happen to him and was afraid to go home to Callie and the rest of his family as a result; instead, he chose to avoid a quick return to Charleston.

Smith also faced a potential problem by remaining in areas under Confederate control. He was a young, able-bodied civilian who was now subject to conscription under the Confederate mobilization law. He had recently been a major, but an encounter with the local provost marshal could result in his becoming a private in a Confederate infantry regiment. After his difficult experiences at the hands of General Floyd when Smith was a field-grade officer, he was understandably reluctant to make a second attempt at an army career as a private.

Smith's luck remained consistently bad. The diary he had been keeping for so long as a long letter to his family, especially to his wife, Callie, fell into Union hands. The N.B. Cabell family may have had their belongings searched at the first checkpoint they crossed. At any rate, the diary was sent directly to General Cox, an officer who knew Isaac Smith's father from the episode with the escaped slave, Mike. He may have shared the information with the Smith family, but the diary itself was retained.

"And they rose in my mind as heroes of the highest magnitude for the spy must of necessity be a noble and courageous character.... How unjust, I thought, that... if captured, that he cannot share even the lot of his fellow captives....Shame on such a law—the spy is a soldier serving his country, a soldier that daily bears the heaviest burdens and risks."

—James E. Taylor

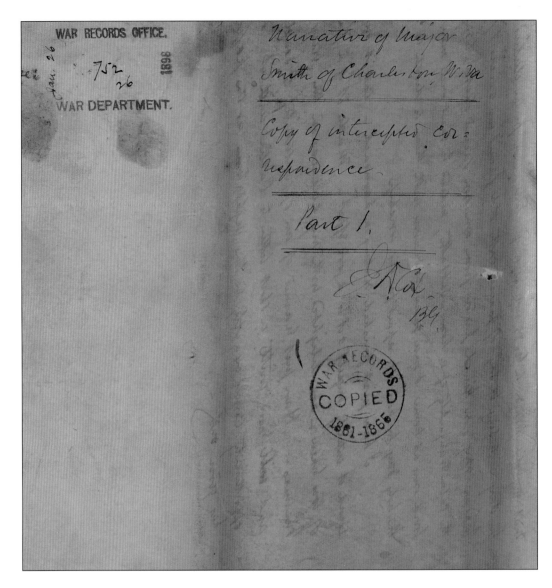

Smith corresponded with his former commander, Colonel Christopher Tompkins, from his temporary residence at the Arbuckle farm in Greenbrier County on November 29, 1861:

The unfortunate position in which I am placed leaves me, I think, no alternative but a return home if such a step is practicable. I cannot participate in any possible way with the government that seeks my father's life & out of the army and its dependencies, see no prospect of earning a livelihood. I am exposed at every moment here to overhear remarks of a most unpleasant character, & am forced to shun society where every member is not my personal acquaintance and friend....The idea of John Clarkson hunting my poor father & mother from their homes (where they have gone I know not where) is beyond endurance. My desire is to unite all the family, & seek some place where we may as far as possible from these civil commotions, live in peace, until the status of the country is settled. It is folly to bring my wife here, we should starve, and more that if I cannot side with my father I will never be his enemy. What is necessary to accomplish my purpose honorably, I scarcely know; it has been a subject of conversation between Mr. Matthews and myself, & I write letters by this mail. If you thought proper to give it, your advice & assistance to my friends would be of great service to me & would make me very grateful. There is difficulty in ascertaining how I should be treated by the enemy upon my return. With Genl Rosecrans I should not fear, feeling assured, he would permit me to return if no [illegible] could be made for my stay. I have no confidence in any of the other officers. I would prefer to stay on this side of the line, but my father's position renders that impossible; so far as my views are concerned, my wish is to occupy as far as practicable, a position of neutrality & bring him to the same platform.

What I have written upon this subject, it is best should be confidential, except to those friends who have or may here-

after undertake to aid me. In truth, I have not yet abandoned the expectation expressed to you just before Floyd arrested me, of finding lodgings in a prison.

Smith had made the crucial decision to attempt to visit his home and family. He stated that he had no fear of General Rosecrans, and so he initiated some correspondence with the Union army's headquarters in order to get home. The Office of the Provost Marshal in Wheeling issued a pass to him in February 1862 that stated "Commanders of Posts, Lines, and Stations; will pass safely into our lines Isaac N. Smith, late a major in the Confederate army, who will report in person immediately to these headquarters to Brigadier W.S. Rosecrans, Comdr Dept. West Va."

There is no evidence that Smith actually kept the appointment to discuss his future with Rosecrans and he wrote another letter to Tompkins from the Arbuckle farm on March 19. He had just heard of the surrender of Fort Donelson, where many of his friends from the Virginia volunteers had been sent under John B. Floyd. John McCausland and the entire 36th Virginia had accompanied the former governor to his new post, where disaster befell them. Floyd had once again managed to escape capture, but he left thousands of Confederate soldiers to accept the terms of U.S. Grant's unconditional surrender. Floyd and the other commander at Fort Donelson, General Pillow, escaped from the Union army, but couldn't escape from Jefferson Davis, who relieved both officers and ordered a court of inquiry. Floyd was at last to face discipline. Smith wrote:

I know how heartily you concur in the action of the President relative to Floyd & Pillow. Floyd's report, garbled as it is, makes but a poor apology for his most remarkable course. How plainly the miserable spirit of the politician appears when contrasted with the chivalry of the soldier, who remained to perform the most painful duty the soldier is ever called to perform, & to shoulder the heavy responsibility, thrust upon him contrary to all rule or decency, by the man who dared not undertake it. How much more pitiful still, the course of Pillow? When he undertakes by forestalling public opinion, in the unauthorized publication of his report, to tarnish the reputation of the officer in captivity that he and Pillow might escape. I regard this passing of command from officer to officer, as nothing less than an order (which it probably was in terms) to an inferior officer. It passed through two politicians, the soldier received it & obeyed; he would have scorned to follow the base example.

At long last, Floyd had been seen for what he was, an unscrupulous politician and a terrible commander who wore the uniform—but possessed none of the qualities—of a general. He and Pillow had fled from doomed Fort Donelson, passing command to Simon Bolivar Buckner, a professional soldier who surrendered the post to his old friend Ulysses S. Grant and went into captivity as Floyd escaped on a steamer that had delivered corn to the fort just prior to the surrender. Pillow was rowed to safety across the Tennessee River in a skiff.

The letter to Tompkins included information about a plan to escape the dilemma facing Smith. He and two others who had resigned from the Confederate army faced two choices: Federal imprisonment if they returned home or a Confederate private's uniform if they remained in eastern Virginia. Fortunately for them, they had found a strong ally, R.M.T. Hunter, recently a U.S. senator and currently a senior member of the Confederate government. Smith wrote:

I have therefore determined to leave for Europe as early as possible, & the original object of this letter was to enquire whether we could not exchange money here, for your drafts upon your agents in Baltimore. Mrs. T and you both have spoken in my presence of means in Baltimore, & your desire to withdraw them. There can hardly be any confiscation of Mrs. T's property & if you would at all be benefited by such an exchange, I think it would be better to take your drafts, & collect from Europe...write to Dr. J.P. Hale (care of James Hunter)

Ulysses S. Grant defeated the incompetent John B. Floyd at Fort Donelson. Floyd, as he had done at Carnifex Ferry and Cotton Hill, fled from the scene to avoid capture by the Federal authorities. Floyd had been indicted in Federal court for questionable activities while secretary of war; as a result, he was concerned that he would be sent to prison if he were ever captured by the Union.

Hanover Junction....Please write Dr. Hale at your first convenience, for if success attends our efforts we hope to get off as early as April 1st. I apprehend great difficulty in getting passports from the Confederate government. Hale and Q----r rely confidently on Mr. James Hunter's efforts through RMT Hunter. We have all three spoken of the pleasure it would afford for you to accompany us, but I can hardly hope you would be willing to leave your family.

Smith's original unit, the Kanawha Riflemen, had been formed from the elite of the small western Virginia town of Charleston and these prominent young men had been friends for many years. The "Hale" of the letter was John Peter Hale, a wealthy physician who had invested heavily in local industry. He organized and paid for the equipment of an artillery battery at the opening of the war, Hale's Battery.

"Q----r" was probably William A. Quarrier, a lieutenant in Hale's battery. Both men had resigned their commissions on the same day, August 21, 1861, and were in the same unfortunate situation as was Isaac Smith. Fortunately, one of them—probably Hale—had a powerful friend in eastern Virginia, James Hunter, the brother of R.M.T. Hunter. The pair's plans to leave the country for Europe were nearly complete.

Smith next wrote to Tompkins to advise that he was moving into eastern Virginia from his temporary lodgings at Arbuckle's farm, near Lewisburg. The Union army was advancing and were expected to capture Lewisburg, so Smith had to move on. He and Quarrier decided to remain together:

In order that we may not become separated as previous arrangements would have required, I have determined to accompany Quarrier to the southwest,

This Confederate disk was used to encode secret messages. First, a key letter was selected and then matched with the letter "A" in the outer ring. Messages were then encrypted by being written with the letters in the inner ring that corresponded with the correct letters in the outer ring. Decoding was accomplished by reversing the process, but the decoder had to know the key letter.

No. 6.   Paris 18th April 1862.

Hon. J. P. Benjamin
          Secretary of State.

                    Sir

                    Referring you to my
my Nº 5 of 14th instant, I have
to report that Mr (h p r u w 2 g
s i k n p g a h) here yesterday and saw
(p x h x y s i.) (i e j x p w g m r e c,)
in response to a note which Mr (j e a h j e j)
had addressed to him stating that he
was charged with an important
message from (t n t v k m u), said
that he could receive no communications
from a foreign power, excepting through
the regular diplomatic channels. The
tone of this response was flippant,
although perhaps intended to be sar-
castic Mr (h m y o k t f) saw Mr
(h z w z s g j k) who expressed great
interest in our affairs and fully
concurred in the views of (s g o x i m n):
he said he had the best reason
to believe that a secret understanding
existed between (s s i h c c t w v s j)
and (v a a b c v,) that (x u k c c v v)
would respect the blockade and with

This coded message to Judah Benjamin may have been encrypted through the use of a "court cypher," a system based on two elements: a key phrase and a twenty-six- by twenty-six-letter grid of the alphabet, called an "alphabet square." Messages encoded in this fashion were almost impossible to decode without knowing the key phrase, making it an extremely reliable system for sending sensitive information.

where he expects to visit his brother, & we will there await advice from Dr. Hale.

I am very much afraid of being entrapped in our efforts to get out. If Va. is abandoned & I am caught in Cottondom unable to get out by land or sea, my misery will be complete.

Two major issues begin to emerge from this series of correspondence with a trusted friend and former commander who apparently felt much the same as Isaac Smith. First, there was serious concern that Virginia could be abandoned to the Union—just as had happened with western Virginia. Second, Smith and Tompkins were lukewarm Rebels, at best. They had become involved in secession out of loyalty to the state of Virginia and they had little love for the politicians of what was referred to as "Cottondom," the deep South that had created the secession crisis. After all, Virginia had joined with the Confederate states when President Lincoln had called for volunteers to suppress the rebellion rather than be a party to the coercion of her sister states.

Smith, in particular, had deep feelings for the concept of a unified nation. He had written with some pangs upon seeing the national flag at the Federal entrenchments on Sewell Mountain. He remained firm in his desire to escape from all the madness of the Civil War, only wanting to sit it out with his loved ones.

Captured Confederates take the oath of allegiance to the Union. Cox opposed the administration of these "test oaths," and as a result, Isaac Smith was not required to be paroled into Union territory when he chose to stay in Charleston. Smith's father and father-in-law posted a cash bond to ensure his "loyalty," and Smith was allowed to move about freely—as he apparently did.

Then Smith received bad news from Dr. Hale and wrote of his disappointment to Tompkins from Marion, Virginia, on April 12:

Dr. Hale having accepted a special commission for a special purpose, from the government, our trip has been postponed, & I regard it abandoned, although the Dr. still has it in view. The change on his part was very unexpected, & somewhat singular under the circumstances, but perfectly innocent on his part, and though it had been a great disappointment to me, I should be unwilling to have him know that the result of his trip to Richmond was so contrary to my expectations. I am still anxious to go....There is said to be no difficulty in leaving from Matamoros.

Hale had accepted a commission from the government for a "special purpose," a phrase that seems to indicate that espionage would be involved. The western Virginians were especially well suited for this type of activity. Accents during that period of history were quite pronounced and those of the western Virginians differed from the accents found in eastern Virginia or the rest of the South. Additionally, the region was partially loyal to the Union and men from that region could pass random security checks easily. Hale and the small party may have found an excellent way to avoid a Federal prison by returning to their homes or a conscription, if they stayed in Confederate territory. Interestingly, when they contacted R.M.T. Hunter, they became of interest to what was to become the Confederate Secret Service Bureau. Hunter, a senior Confederate official, was entrusted with at least a part of the Secret Service fund. Now, a group of potential agents had entered into his ring of influence and one, a doctor who had extensive business interests in western Virginia, had entered into their clandestine service.

Isaac Smith would soon be offered a similar opportunity to return to the service of Virginia. The offer would come from Christopher Tompkins, a man whom he trusted, who had also been offered an opportunity to help his "Native State" (the fact that Tompkins' wife had stated that he would do anything for his state in one of her letters may have led to Tompkins' induction into the secret service.

Smith had an opportunity to send a letter to Tompkins through a trusted mutual friend. In this hand-carried letter, Smith revealed his true feelings about his situation:

Mr. Dryden's visit to Richmond affords me an opportunity of writing more freely than I care to do by mail. But for the prevalence of martial law, I should probably return to Greenbriar & enjoy the comfortable home I had formed there. When located again (& all thought of the European trip abandoned) I shall not retreat from the enemy's approach, my comfort and purse but illy affords such flights. Located near the center of the state if the government abandons it, I shall not feel it my duty to go further. It is impossible for me to remain much longer in uncertainty about my wife. All communication is cut off, & at this moment I cannot tell whether she is dead or alive. A great difficulty stares men in the face, in the conscription law. My determination as to entering the service is fixed—like yourself I feel acquitted of further obligations to my state. I have given up everything man holds dear, & in return have met with insult and brutality from an officer whose authority I never intended to acknowledge, when I entered the service, &

whose private and public character has always commanded my strong contempt. My state would give me no redress—I would not ask it from any other source. In this feeling, there was much that influenced me in refusing to demand a court of inquiry. I have never said so much to you before. If pressed by the conscription law I am in hopes with what money & property I have here & can command, exemption may be purchased by substitution, but if forced to extremities, unless some other mode of escape can be secured, I shall frankly state my views & go to prison. I am full to overflowing on the subject of the war, the government & matters generally, but will say nothing more...& looking upon political matters with more or less distrust I do my utmost to keep my tongue still, lest my speech offend others or put myself into difficulty—the same feelings made me shun society in Richmond.

Even as Smith wrote this letter, however, another way of escaping his dilemma was forming in other quarters. Smith moved from Marion, Virginia, to live with a relative five miles (8km) south of Staunton, Virginia. During that time, several letters were sent to him from Tompkins in very short order—on April 18, 20, and 22—the first two going to Marion and the third to Lewisburg. Tompkins was trying to contact Smith as quickly as possible with an offer that could solve his problem with the Conscription Act.

John McCausland had been in contact with Tompkins and had a proposal for Tompkins and Smith. This is referred to in Smith's letters as only "McCausland's idea," but it involved travel to Canada, where the Confederacy maintained a robust espionage establishment. Smith wrote to Tompkins on May 1, 1862:

Under these circumstances it is impossible for me to discuss fully the propositions of your letter relative to the journey. McCausland's idea at present best suits my fancy, but if successful I should stop in Canada.

Smith was trying to arrange a trip in safety from Staunton to Lewisburg to meet with his minister from Charleston, a man who had some news of Smith's family. As anxious as he was to learn of the welfare of his family, he had to cancel his travel plans:

My hope of seeing Dr. Broun has been frustrated & I have been obliged to cancel the trip to Lewisburg.

The imprudence of my coming to Richmond is more evident than ever. In this part of the country there is no safety for travelers, even along neighborhood roads. Men travel about & arrest any citizen they meet without regard to law, and carry the prisoners to the army. You, of course, would be subject to no such danger, but a quiet retinacy is my only safety. Until a few days since, the country from Staunton to Lewisburg offered every facility for the test of McCausland's idea—it is not much changed now. Could you run up to Staunton & consult on the subject of your letters to me?

Again, Smith mentions his preoccupation with his fear of being arrested and impressed into the Confederate army as a private. He also mentions "McCausland's idea" a second time, a plan that would result in Smith's remaining in Canada, if he were successful. The "idea" was something that Smith didn't choose to discuss in a letter that could be read by someone other than the addressee and he asked Tompkins to come to Staunton, in person, to discuss the plan.

Smith was concerned that his mail might be monitored and wrote: "My letters have not been sent to me. I have some suspicion that they have been detained by military authority, but I hope this is a mistake."

Letters from his wife had to pass through the lines of confrontation and were read by Confederate censors prior to being released for delivery. (A similar system was in place for mail entering Union territory; the Federal censor was future president Rutherford B. Hayes.) Smith was quite anxious to get letters from home; he wrote Tompkins that "an event which was looked for in March, has resulted in giving me a son." Now, he

had an additional reason to worry about his future.

Smith was, however, still willing to proceed with "McCausland's idea" and wrote to Tompkins that he was willing to test the idea in the territory between Staunton and Lewisburg. This operational testing plan, his reluctance to discuss the details of the plan in a letter, and Smith's intention to remain in Canada if he were successful all point to clandestine activity. Shortly before Tompkins approached Smith with this tentative plan, Dr. Hale had reentered Confederate service with a "special commission for a special purpose" and had developed an indirect rela-

Miners such as these provided the coal and iron needed by the Tredegar Arms Works in Richmond. Christopher Tompkins managed the factories' coal operation in nearby Goochland County.

tionship with R.M.T. Hunter, a Confederate government official who had specific authority to extend payments from Secret Service funds. There is every indication that Tompkins was also involved in clandestine activity from his new commercial responsibilities at the coal mines in Goochland County, mines that provided coal for the Tredegar Works, the major arms factory in Richmond. After a period of assessment through letters, Tompkins had probably requested authority from his superiors to recruit his friend and former subordinate for an espionage mission. Smith was taking the offer seriously and even suggested operational testing of the concept prior to deployment. These men were intelligent, skilled college graduates and combat veterans who were beginning a new enterprise that held substantial risk for them. Needless to say, they were not approaching it as a sort of schoolboy lark.

Smith wrote an excellent analysis of the military situation in a letter to Tompkins dated July 17, 1862. The Confederate army was preparing to move north, perhaps into Union territory, and Smith was concerned about the outcome, if the northern population was to be aroused to a greater degree than it was already:

I believe the time to carry out the purpose spoken of more favorable now than ever heretofore; & that after the movement now contemplated by the army assembling here, the difficulties & dangers will be greatly increased. The Government heeding the cry for the invasion of the enemy's country evidently intended to push a column into Pennsylvania or Maryland, most probably the former. In my opinion, the time for this movement has passed; the column will be too far advanced beyond the base of defense & from re-inforcements, it could be attacked in flank and rear at any point from Harrisonburg northward; it will have to draw its supplies from too distant a point; & whilst Jackson may make a foray & a successful one, he must be forced back very rapidly. The consequences of such an incursion I can scarcely conceive; you who have witnessed the temper & spirit of our soldiery in the western campaigns, & from the character of the army (Texans, Mississippians &c) now serving here, can form an appropriate idea of the course they would adopt in the enemy's country. The North will be aroused & exasperated to an extent hitherto unknown, & the war from that time forward will become a war of savage barbarity on both sides. At an earlier period, the South might possibly have been perfectly willing the war should assume such a character, but with the enemy controlling & occupying seven states, & enough of the remaining six to make one large state, the experiment is at least hazardous if not fatal.

The occupying and invading Yankee armies will not only commit such excesses as they have already committed, but they will exceed if possible the outrages attributed to them so freely by the papers, for the purpose of firing the soldier's zeal in the Southern cause. The temper of the people & the army now is to respect nothing in the enemy's country neither property, age or sex. Devastation & fires will mark their course. The country expects-and demands this of them, & they will not be slow to gratify the country in their wish. I have no idea that a Southern army can occupy Northern territory; they can only enter it & retire after inflicting all the injury they possibly can. Occupying the advanced position Jackson will have to do, retreat is inevitable. His last advance shows that fact—his army was strong enough to check Fremont & Shields together, but he was forced to retreat to Port Republic before he could fight. Until he reached that place his flanks and rear were not secure.

Under the circumstances I fear the course I have determined to pursue will be too unsafe. There are other causes too operating very strongly to make it necessary I should make some change. I have always believed in the feasibility of McCausland's suggestions, but should choose a different direction, in which its accomplishment would be very easy. I am very much concerned & unhappy & would give a great deal for a short interview with you, but cannot meet you. I have no definite plan in view & ask if you adopt any course relative to these matters, I beg you to give me an opportunity to join you.

It appears that a part of the plan outlined by McCausland may have involved Smith and others to follow the army as it moved forward and remain in place as it withdrew. They may have been able to pose as local residents prior to moving on inside Federal territory or they may have stated plainly to Federal officers that they were resigned Confederate officers seeking to avoid conscription, a cover story that was so close to reality that it would be accepted at face value. Once inside Federal territory, they could move on to Charleston where Smith's father would be able to use his Unionist influence to shield them as they performed covert duties for the Confederate government.

Dr. Hale, by virtue of the "special commission," was able to travel in Confederate territory, and met with Tompkins in Richmond prior to returning to remain with Smith. In a letter written to Tompkins on

July 2, Smith wrote: "Dr. H tells me you saw my recent letters to him, & are much disposed to pursue the same course, if at all admissible by the situation of your family."

Another letter, with cryptic references to travel and passports, was sent to Tompkins on July 23. They had initiated the plan that involved Smith, Tompkins, and Dr. Hale. Tompkins and Hale could travel freely, but Smith was having some serious problems. He wrote:

I meet difficulty with the first increment. The Provost-marshal here gives a pass to everyone who goes on the cars & examines them as to liability to service &c before the pass is given. The private and public roads are scoured by the provost guard who question and arrest every man in the county liable to service. I see wagon loads of men, taken by the door here every day or two, many of them tied and handcuffed. These difficulties of mine neither you nor the Dr. seem to appreciate. If you could be with me, the application for passports might be made by you in my absence and my title (defunct as it is) might save me. I will telegraph you also. Shall I come down or can you come up & help me off? Telegraph your reply to James G. Cochran, Staunton, who goes to town for me & attends to this matter.

I most earnestly entreat you not to act without me. Had I received your letter at the proper time I should have been at Charlottesville at the appointed time. I should most heartily & bitterly deplore any action on your part which I could not be permitted to share.

Tompkins and Hale were in the process of initiating their plan and Smith was apparently about to miss their reunion at the starting point where passports would be

obtained. They were either preparing to depart for the safety of a foreign country or all three were to begin a journey that would conclude in a foreign country—as had been outlined in "McCausland's idea." Whether Tompkins was about to go to safety or into mortal danger, it is obvious that his friend, Isaac Smith was determined to go along with him.

Smith included a postscript written on September 2 that set the trip into motion: "Have just learned that Loring's force had received orders—the cavalry to go to Cumberland Gap. If so I shall expect to see you at once."

General Pope, commander of the Army of the Potomac, had lost his letterbook containing copies of all of his correspondence. From it Lee learned that Pope had ordered General Cox to move his Kanawha Division from the vicinity of Charleston to unite with the Army of the Potomac. Once Lee was aware of Cox's planned movement, he sent orders to William W. Loring to move against the small residual Union force occupying the strategic Kanawha Valley. Lee wrote "I deem

The men of the 22nd and 36th Virginia, as with many infantrymen of the Civil War (particularly on the Confederate side), achieved some remarkable feats of perambulation. Even such poorly equipped Confederate soldiers as those shown in this illustration were capable of extraordinary efforts. Indeed, the men of the "Stonewall" Brigade referred to themselves as "foot cavalry" because of the great distances they covered in their marches.

it important that General Loring should be informed of the force opposed to him and directed to clear the valley of the Kanawha and then operate northwardly, so as to join me in the Valley of Virginia."

The movement of the Confederate cavalry sent to screen Loring's army was detected by Isaac Smith, who probably wrote "I shall expect to see you at once" because the first movement of Confederate troops into the Kanawha Valley was the signal to finally implement "McCausland's idea."

Subsequent correspondence from Smith (once he was positioned in Charleston) to Tompkins (near Richmond) advised that the horse and saddle loaned to the former major had been sent to the Arbuckle farm for Tompkins' recovery and that Smith was planning to remain with his family as the Union army reoccupied the area. Cox entered Charleston on October 29 and Smith remained there to be interviewed as a former Confederate officer. His father and father-in-law both posted a bond for him and he was not required to take an "oath of allegiance" to the U.S. government as Cox felt such oaths were "useless." Smith had managed to get his wish and he was now residing with his family in relative safety.

There is a gap in the correspondence record between these two, Smith now inside Federal territory and Tompkins at Richmond; the next letter recovered is dated February 18, 1863. Smith had been corresponding through the Federal mail system with Ellen Tompkins, now in Baltimore. The letter reveals a great deal of additional information about their activities at this time. Ellen was at No. 7 Cathedral Street in Baltimore and Smith had hoped to be able to travel there to meet with her.

Smith sent his letters through the Dixie Mail, the underground delivery system by which letters were smuggled through enemy lines. Smith wrote from Charleston and the

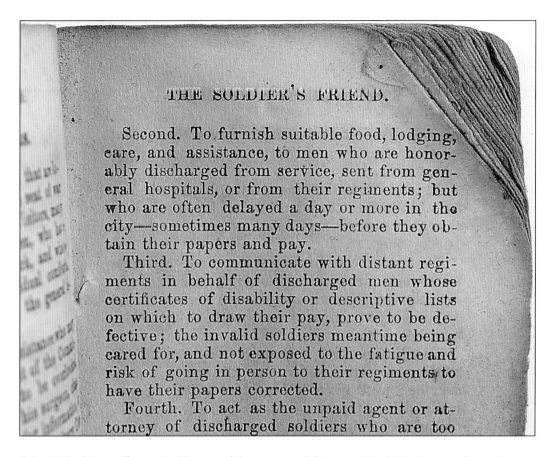

"The Soldier's Friend" contained listings of their responsibilities in special situations, such as when they were honorably discharged or paroled from enemy captivity.

letters were delivered securely and quickly. In this latest letter, Smith reveals that Dr. Hale had joined the others in Charleston and that "Dr. H hopes to be able to meet her, he has gone to the western states & will visit New York before his return, & Baltimore also if Mrs. T is there when he is in the east." The former Confederate officer was actively traveling throughout Federal territory for what appears to be commercial reasons. Hale was involved in a steamboat operation in upper New York during 1863 and he remained in close contact with Smith in Charleston. Smith and some others with whom he was associated were also traveling and Tompkins, as related by Smith, was well aware of the results:

Meehan is here & is well but fretting, of course. His great difficulty lies, I think, in his excitable temperament. I have heard that a passport was promised him (during my absence) & Meehan talked so much on the subject that it was deemed imprudent to permit him to go, lest his want of caution rather than want of integrity, might prove prejudicial. This was told me by Meehan's friends & my own since my return. It may, or may not, be correct. Meehan's only difficulty is his inability to get to Richmond, he is under no other restraint, but is much annoyed. You recollect a trip he made to the country & its results; he is eager to continue so suc-

Veterans on furlough often went home for a short break (for instance, during the winter when there was infrequent combat), where they were able to tell spellbinding stories about their camp and battlefield experiences to a public largely unfamiliar with combat on the scale of the Civil War.

cessful a beginning, & it is grieving him to know he can't. Dr. H and I think this weighs more heavily on his mind than anything.

There are clear indications of espionage in this paragraph. Meehan had made a successful trip and wanted to return to Richmond in order to start another. He had been promised a passport but had talked about his mission in some way and the person in charge, possibly Hale, had halted the operation rather than risk exposure. Smith had been out of the state—also on an operation of some type—and he and Dr. Hale were back together once again.

Unfortunately, no additional letters of this type were located. Tompkins kept a detailed diary during 1863, but a close examination reveals little. His handwriting is so poor that only he could read all of it; but his handwriting was legible in letters written to George Washington Collum, who was preparing a register of West Point graduates, in 1855.

Curiously, one researcher, unaware of the possible connection of Tompkins to the Confederate Secret Service Bureau, felt that Tompkins had "written to deceive" when he made his entries into the diary.

As tantalizing as it is to speculate about the actual missions undertaken by the Confederate spies in McCausland's group of agents, without evidence such speculation would be guesswork. On the one hand, it is frustrating to know so much about these men of the Civil War and yet to have so little information about their actual activities once they had agreed to spy in the name of the Confederacy. On the other hand, however, the diary that Major Isaac N. Smith kept is in itself a document of espionage in the sense that it was written from a most critical point of view, almost as if Smith were a double agent, and because it was captured by Union forces and no doubt served to give them insight into the workings of the Confederate power structure within the Virginia theater. Of course, the document was as critical as it was because of the great unhappiness Smith and his men experienced under the command of the incompetent and vengeful commander John B. Floyd. And, of course, Smith and others like him were driven to spy because their options—imprisonment or conscription as a private—were hardly options at all.

Colonel of the Cofederacy, *by Don Troiani, shows an officer of the Rebel army. Typically, even the infantry commanders wore the gear associated with a horseman; note the knee-high riding boots, complete with spurs, on this colonel.*

EPILOGUE

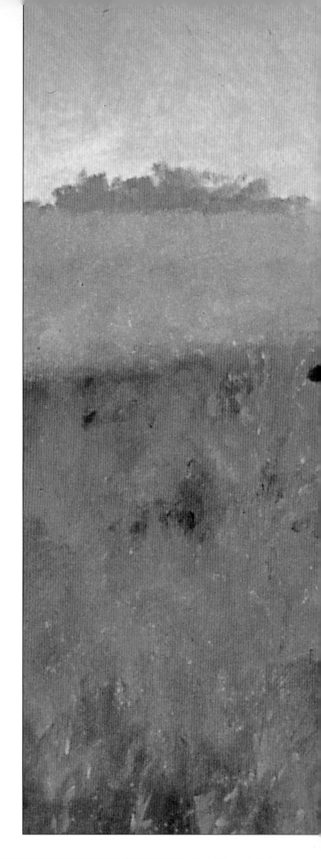

The final clue about the activities of these Confederate agents from 1863 until the end of the war is provided by Tompkins in a narrative he prepared describing the fall of Richmond. He wrote about the arrival of Governor Smith and his son, Bell, at his home. After they had been fed and rested, they left for Lynchburg. Later Tompkins told of another Confederate in need of help:

I had not the heart to send him away on foot, but gave him a mule & put a boy upon another to carry him to the R. Road. The boy came back the next day, minus the mules. Mr. Baxter took him to Flat Rock & the boy started back & got two miles [3km] when he met a soldier who dismounted him & in a note to me politely informed me the Yankees were close upon his track & he regretted the necessity of pressing my mules, but must do it, signing himself, naively enough Jas. N. Snead, singularly enough the initials Isaac N. Smith.

Colonel Tompkins rightly considered it naive of Isaac Noyes Smith to have chosen to use the alias Jas. N. Snead because the new name had identical initials as his true name. A spy with nearly three years of experience in carrying out "McCausland's idea" should certainly have known better.

Confederate reconnaissance operations were very successful during the early stages of the war. Raised as hunters and horsemen, southern soldiers adapted more quickly to military life than their more urban northern counterparts.

along the breastworks, the
at their posts — The position
some time before & I rode in
position, hitched my horse,

It was the opinion of n
that the enemy would not
but would simply annoy us
train passed down the road
Bridge & would then follow t
position. I will try to giv
like New river runs between t
with high ranges of cliffs on